Praise for
When Paradise Speaks

When Paradise Speaks reminds me of the bestselling book, *Eat, Pray, Love* with the addition of spiritual companions from the afterlife. It is a true story about three friends, a sudden death, and after-death communication from the deceased friend and other spiritual guides who offer amazing guidance about our lives both here on Earth and on the other side. Their messages from the afterlife also inspired the stunning Lovitude™ Soul Paintings that grace the pages of this book and have been called Visual Blessings.

I highly recommend going through this journey with Risë and Anne. It will impact you in ways you can't imagine.

—**Echo Bodine,**
author of *Echoes of the Soul* and
A Still, Small Voice

It has been proven that in reading or hearing others' experiences, we open ourselves to these and greater experiences. You hold in your hands a most excellent account of love, connection, and eternal life that has the potential to transform you in unimaginable ways.

Your book, Risë and Anne, will be a gift to many.

—**Suzanne Giesemann,**
author of *Messages of Hope*

When Paradise Speaks is a remarkable, true story about an individual's spiritual journey. Risë Severson Kasmirski connects with guides and loved ones in the afterlife who long to support us in this life to live our best life, while bringing light and love to others. It is written in a language that is both informative and conversational, authentically coming from the heart.

Risë has done a brilliant job of integrating spiritual principles with real-life experiences, modeling the wisdom of being open to new learnings and experiences with positive benefits for all. The continuous profound question she asks is: "What is the lesson here?"

Anne Pryor has been on a parallel journey following her intuition, while connecting with Spirit and being open to guidance from the other side. Although Anne did not train as an artist, her soul paintings are making a profound impact in the world. The inclusion of her Spirit- inspired-work makes this book a real treasure.

—Louise Griffith, MA,
founder of One Shining Light, and
author of *You Are Worth It: 52 Weeks to Honoring,
Loving and Nurturing Your Soul*

What a magnificent book! The author takes us on an intriguing journey of divine encounters with the afterlife through conversations with a friend who has passed and other spirit guides. Their great wisdom is available to us all if we will only open ourselves to it.

I read this book a few days after my mother had passed. Divine timing, indeed! While I already believed that my mother is *still right here*, the messages and love on the pages helped me center into that place of peace, which surpasses all understanding.

—Jana Bauer,
author of *Sun and Moon:
Chronicles of a Stepfamily*

When Paradise Speaks has the power to transform your relationship with the afterlife. In this true story, Risë shares her profound experiences in communicating with her deceased friend, one whose death came too early. Risë's subsequent inner journey through meditation and other spiritual experiences lead her to new insights, understanding, and gifts, far beyond what she could have imagined.

As her guide through a year of deep meditation and spiritual coaching, I witnessed Risë's curiosity, self- doubt, intense learning, and acceptance of the spiritual messages that ultimately manifested into the book you are holding. Anne Pryor's Lovitude™ Soul Paintings, found throughout the book, were also inspired through after-death communication with the same deceased friend. These vibrant paintings elicit deep feelings of spiritual connection and joy.

—**Wes Hamilton,**
Spiritual Life Leadership Coach,
Master Numerologist, Co-President of Core Passion™

When Paradise Speaks is a fascinating story about encounters with the afterlife. Risë and Anne's incredible experiences remind us to ask for messages, pay attention, and be ready to be amazed! Risë is a captivating storyteller that will keep you on the edge of your seat.

—**Patrick Pryor, M.Div., BCC**

WHEN PARADISE SPEAKS

Ask & Allow,
In Love & Gratitude,
Risë & Janie

WHEN PARADISE SPEAKS

A REMARKABLE, TRUE STORY OF FRIENDSHIP,
AFTER-DEATH COMMUNICATION,
AND ART THAT HEALS

Risë Severson Kasmirski

LOVITUDE SOUL PAINTINGS BY ANNE PRYOR

Library of Congress Cataloging-in-Publication Data When paradise speaks: the remarkable, true story of friendship, after-death communication, and art that heals / by Risë Severson Kasmirski, with Lovitude Soul Paintings by Anne Pryor.

Library of Congress Number: 2020920995

ISBN 978-1-7352920-0-7 (paperback)
ISBN 978-1-7352920-1-4 (eBook)

Published in the United States of America

OCCO22000 BODY, MIND & SPIRIT / Afterlife & Reincarnation
OCCO03000 BODY, MIND & SPIRIT / Channeling & Mediumship
OCCO32009 BODY, MIND & SPIRIT / Angels & Spirit Guides
OCCO27000 BODY, MIND & SPIRIT / Spiritualism
OCCO19000 BODY, MIND & SPIRIT / Inspiration & Personal Growth

Publisher: Lovitude Publishing—lovitude.com
Editor: Nina Shoroplova—NinaShoroplova.ca
Book Interior and eBook Design: Amit Dey—amitdey2528@gmail.com
Publishing Consultant: Geoff Affleck—geoff@geoffaffleck.com

Contents

Prologue

When *Paradise Speaks* is an inspiring story of deep friendship, after-death communication and the remarkable events that occurred following the sudden passing of my friend, Irene. It is a true story about a trio of friends—Irene, Anne, and me—and how we built a deep spiritual connection over the two years following Irene's death. The gifts Anne and I received through the clear and inspiring messages Irene communicated to us from the afterlife leave us knowing that our loved ones who pass are always with us.

Friends for more than two decades, Irene and I were coworkers, confidantes, travel companions, and great friends. We loved to analyze politics, chat about celebrities and royalty, and share our lifelong passion for movies and travel. I was devastated when she died.

Immediately after Irene passed, I began to feel her presence around me. The first time I *saw* her, I was giving a eulogy at her memorial service and I was certain that she was sitting in a front-row bench off to the side of the synagogue. She was smiling and glancing over the congregation, her long, auburn hair reflecting light from the windows towering above. I was sure that my mind was playing tricks on me. That day was followed by many sightings of Irene over several months and lucid dreams that began within three months of her passing, as I describe in depth in chapter one.

Throughout the first year following her death, I filled several journals with the lucid dreams and channeled messages from Irene that were consistently filled with love and hope for those of us she left behind.

Messages from Irene to Anne and Me

One year after her death, Irene encouraged me to write this book about our journey and share it with the world. She did this by communicating with me through a session I experienced with a medium, an intermediary who provides communication to the living from someone who has passed. It is Irene's desire that this story be told, and action be taken on the messages I received.

A few weeks after my session, through the same medium, Irene shared specific instructions with Anne to begin creating bold, "peacock-colored paintings" using a unique process involving ink, large sheets of plastic, and her breath. Irene advised Anne to share these images with the world.

The irony is that Anne was not an artist, nor was Irene, but within months Anne had created hundreds of stunning pieces of art that she calls Lovitude™ Soul Paintings, using the unique process described by Irene. As time went by, and through ongoing communication with Irene, I was able to provide additional directions to Anne on how to further enhance the paintings. Anne has demonstrated her painting technique on the Hallmark Home and Family show, and her images are printed on greeting cards, pillows, wall hangings, and many other products marketed worldwide with a significant portion of the earnings donated to charities.

After-Death Communication—What Research Tells Us

What happens when we die? Does our spirit leave our body at death? and if so, where does our spirit go? Can our spirit come back to communicate with us? And, if so, why does hardly anyone talk about these things?

Anne and I have pondered these questions our entire lives.

The term After-Death Communication (ADC), coined by Bill and Nancy Guggenheim in the 1980s, describes the interactions individuals have with deceased friends and relatives in the spirit world.

In their groundbreaking research of three thousand individuals worldwide, and in their subsequent book *Hello from Heaven: A New Field of Research ~ After-Death Communication Confirms that Life and Love Are Eternal*, the Guggenheims concluded that an estimated 25 percent to 40 percent of the population believe they have been contacted by a loved one who has passed away, sometimes years after their loved one departed.

Yet, we do not hear many of these stories. People seem hesitant to speak of their ADC experiences, perhaps thinking that these communications are products of their active imagination or simply wishful thinking.

Through their research, the Guggenheims identified ten universally common ways people report that the spirit world communicates with them. These include through one of the five senses: hearing the voice of a loved one, seeing a partial or full human form, sensing energy around them, smelling a familiar scent, or tasting something that triggers a memory of their loved one.

Other common forms of ADC include specific birds swooping overhead more often than usual (for instance, cardinals and eagles are often reported), feathers showing up in unlikely places, coins appearing more often than usual (finding pennies and dimes on the ground), and through sequences of numbers materializing repeatedly (for example, 111, 7, 11).

As anecdotal evidence, have we not all heard stories from people about randomly finding pennies on the ground, and the person's grandmother immediately coming to mind? Or seeing a cardinal at the most unlikely times, reminding them that their loved one is nearby?

ADC Is Available to Everyone

It is not necessary that you practice a religion or even believe in an afterlife to follow along on this journey. The three of us—Irene, Anne, and I—were raised with different religious backgrounds, but this had no impact on the loving messages Anne and I received from across the thin veil between this world and the next. All religions honor a powerful, loving presence that we refer to as God in this story.

We invite you to consider that a vast world exists beyond what our five senses tell us is real. If we are open to new possibilities and keep our skeptical egoic mind out of the way, amazing things can happen. This book is proof.

Communicating with the Spirit World

Much of the book you are about to read comprises verbatim journal entries from my after-death communications with Irene. I invite you to read these sections as though you yourself are having a conversation with a good friend. You will notice that she calls me by my nickname *Reese* throughout this story.

Occasionally you will find incomplete sentences, random thoughts, and puzzling word choices. Because spirit often communicates through symbolism and metaphor, it might be difficult to make sense of the messages being presented. I learned to quickly write down the messages as I received them, without slowing down to try to interpret their meaning. Have patience with yourself. The story unfolds and the hidden meanings in these messages become clearer over time.

You will also encounter journal entries from another voice that I call "Coach" (more on Coach later) that intermingle with those from Irene to support content and meaning of the messages.

Lovitude™ Soul Paintings and Photographs

Sprinkled throughout the book are several Lovitude Soul Paintings from Anne's vast collection. Each painting was created and named by Anne, and each name holds a special meaning. At the back of the book is a resource list of online sites you can visit to see more of her beautiful work.

All photographs displayed throughout the book were taken by either me or Anne.

Irene is Present

Anne and I see evidence everywhere that Irene's generous spirit is present, and that she and others from the spirit world want to communicate with us and through us. She sits with me as I write these words and is nudging me to be honest and open and forthright in what she is telling me to say to you. She wants to help write the book—she tells me she is *my ghostwriter … my pen pal from the other side*. I am the scribe, Anne is the artist, and Irene is directing us both.

We tell this story to assure you that ADC is real and connection with the spirit world is our birthright. We will share ways that you might access messages, comfort, and support from your loved ones who have passed.

Ultimately, we believe a powerful loving force surrounds and lives through all of us, and we are all here to do our highest and greatest good. The spirit world *is* paradise and speaks to us in so many ways if we are only willing to listen.

Blessings,
Risë and Anne

*"**Paradise Speaks**: Everywhere the voice of God and angels and guides. Pennies from heaven, the whisper of the wind, a voice that will not let you rest, a sense to go this way or that, a shimmer of light, sound in the quiet night. We are always here for you."* —COACH

A definition of the name Irene: "Fun, smart, beautiful, and gets along with others! She is the type of person you go to for advice. Irene is the motherly type. But don't mess with her. She's one tough cookie!" Urban Dictionary

Always Beside You

THE BEGINNING

Paradise

Chapter 1

Costa Rica—Heaven on Earth

A Warm Tropical Paradise

New Year's Eve at 3:15 a.m. Wide awake hours before dawn on this numbingly cold Minnesota morning, I am showered, and dressed in stretchy, forgiving yoga pants, t-shirt, sweatshirt, jacket, gloves, and wool socks under my sandals. Swimsuits and active wear are packed for the week and I am ready to go. Excitement courses through me as I contemplate seven glorious days in the warm tropical paradise of Costa Rica.

I am on my way to the Blue Spirit Resort in the town of Nosara, located in the northwest corner of Costa Rica. The resort, created by a co-founder of the Omega Institute, Stephan Rechtschaffen, MD, is a world-class yoga and meditation retreat center. It is nestled on a hilltop in the jungle overlooking the Pacific Ocean with thirteen stunning miles of sandy beach stretching out in both directions. Anne, my trusted friend, and colleague of several years has coerced me into attending a weeklong "gentle" yoga retreat. Though I do not practice yoga, nor does Anne, I caved in just weeks ago and said yes to her invitation, "gentle" being the pivotal word to lure me in.

Anne likes to coax me to step outside my comfort zone. I know that if I disengage from work from time to time, I can center and ground myself once again, which is good for the professional side of me. Less stress—more progress. I know it will be a challenging week, and I also hope that it will be a deeply nurturing and relaxing experience. Anything is better than facing the bleak early days of January back home in Minnesota, where the godforsaken winter cold is deep in my bones and will not lessen its grip.

Anne's brother Patrick has come along with us to escape the cold and keep us entertained with his deadpan humor and endless antics. A mild-mannered hospice chaplain, he has subtle, silly humor that catches us off guard. Sometimes, during yoga class, he merely glances at us from across the room with a certain quirky expression and we erupt into peals of laughter that we struggle to stifle. This creates a sharp contrast to the meditative atmosphere surrounding us and we are suddenly schoolchildren about to be reprimanded.

Patrick is a welcome addition to our party. He practices yoga at a local gym and is expert at knowing how to modify yoga poses to help us maintain our dignity. The more experienced and, frankly, younger students around us practice graceful postures that make us want to slink out of class when no one is looking. Each morning we meet for yoga class at the crack of dawn, then again in the late afternoon, so we have many opportunities to feel inadequate while we strive for deep relaxation.

Throughout the week, Patrick takes an interest in everyone and is quick to engage others in conversation. He tells Anne and me with a coy smile "I listen hard and ask lots of questions, so I don't have to talk about myself." The women love him. Mr. Congeniality is sought after by many, including the self-proclaimed *oldest* woman at the resort with her wild curly hair and oversized brightly rimmed glasses that dwarf her minuscule frame. She keeps him mildly entertained with her moxie and her endless tales of world travels.

Blue Spirit Resort

Blue Spirit Resort is only sixty-some miles from the airport, yet it takes us more than two hours to arrive. We are packed like sardines into an uncomfortably warm van, traversing the pocked and bumpy gravel roads. Seatbelts barely hold us in place as we jostle along, holding on tight while the wheels of the van lunge into ruts in the road. There are eleven of us packed into a van that fits eight comfortably and we do our best to pass the time through conversation and shared snacks. Our driver is oblivious to our discomfort.

We travel a short distance on a paved highway and then we are on rural country roads the rest of the way. Barefoot children play in the sand outside small wooden houses, shacks in some cases. They wave to us as we go by, sometimes chasing after the van as they laugh with delight. Occasionally there are animals standing in the road—oxen, pigs, chickens—with no urgency to move. The sky is a bright blue backdrop to vibrant tropical flowers and trees, and in the heat of this climate, we are grateful to have already stripped off our heavy winter layers.

Despite how hot and tired we are, it is well worth the trip when we finally arrive. As the van inches up the steep, winding road through the resort to the main lodge, I know I have never been in such a magnificent place. This is paradise—heaven on earth! We are in a Blue Zone, one of only a few places on earth where people routinely live to be over a hundred years old. The sheer beauty surrounding me makes me instantly understand how this could be so.

There are canopies of lush tree branches and lovely palm trees that provide much-needed shade for the small huts that house visitors and yoga classes just down the hill from the main lodge. Foliage in a million variations of verdant green. Bright tropical birds. An infinity pool tucked behind palm trees, with clear, refreshing water endlessly cascading into the jungle below. This place is alive with the tropical sounds of insects and exotic bird. Agile monkeys traverse throughout the jungle.

In the main lodge, perched on top of the hill, the open-air lobby and dining room are covered with a massive thatched roof that blends into the natural surroundings. A gentle, warm breeze flows through the lobby. Terracotta tiles feel cool to bare feet. There are rustic wooden tables where I will share vegetarian breakfasts, lunches, and dinners with other resort guests, made from only the most natural, freshest ingredients. With my disdain for raw fish, strange beans, and unfamiliar vegetables, I am secretly grateful for my private stash of trail mix and M&M's to help me through this week.

Surrounding the dining area, rattan couches and chairs with their overstuffed pillows in bright tropical designs form relaxing conversation areas for guests. Throughout the day and late into the evening, small groups will gather in deep conversation and quiet laughter against a backdrop of the dark jungle. Native sculptures, ceramics, and woven wall hangings remind me that I am far from home.

Just one step down from the lobby and dining area, I am walking on lush green grasses with a stunning panoramic view of a landscape that is alive with sound and movement. To the west, the Pacific Ocean stretches out to the horizon. The beach can be accessed by walking down more than a hundred well-worn wooden steps just off the lobby, past the small guest huts, yoga studios, and a large tent where some of the guests sleep. Then onto the rugged winding trail that meanders down the steep hill leading to the beach. My senses are happily on overload as I survey the beauty around me.

The resort is filled with guests attending other yoga retreats, and attentive resort staff help us with our every need. The Costa Ricans may be the friendliest people I've ever met. They pause when engaged in conversation. Listen carefully. Maintain eye contact. Say *please* and *thank you*, *what do you need?* and *how can I help?* Twice I experience a staff member gently scooping up a palm-size tropical bug that has wandered into the dining area. "Don't step on it!" they shout to me (as if I would!) as they carefully set it free in the outdoors.

The week passes quickly, one day melting into the next. There is no need for a clock—we are on jungle time. The tropical birds and wild monkeys sing their morning and evening songs to mark the passing days.

I journal and meditate daily. Practice yoga poses. Lounge with a handful of other guests at the infinity pool with quick dips into the cool and refreshing water. Eat every kind of vegetation imaginable and fall into deep sleep as soon as the sun goes down.

I have opted to stay in one of the small, rustic guest rooms in the main lodge and am instantly grateful for that decision. On the

Blue Spirit Resort, upper yoga studio

second floor, my bed faces a large screened window that separates me from the jungle. Each morning, I am jolted awake in the pitch dark, right before dawn, to the screeching of howler monkeys perched among the trees. They are right outside my jungle tree-house and their screams to one another are punctuated by long pauses of stunning silence that mesmerizes me for the half-hour or so until the sun appears on the horizon.

Each day I sink deeper and deeper into total relaxation and it feels divine. Everything about this tropical paradise melts my stress away. I have a makeup-free face, wild untamable hair, and I no longer care that I am appalling at yoga. I want to stay here forever.

A Walk to the Ocean

Five days after I arrive, it is Thursday and I am taking my first solo walk down the winding sand and gravel path to the ocean. It is late morning and I have been up since 5:00 a.m. to meditate, attend yoga class, eat fresh fruits and hearty breads, and drink rich, potent coffee. I have free time until the late afternoon class and I meander slowly down the uneven wooden steps, then the steep hill, soaking in the spectacular nature and jungle sounds that surround me. It is another hot, humid day in paradise.

The jungle is alive with the pitched hum of the cicadas, crickets, and other unnamed insects. Spiders drape colossal webs from tree branch to tree branch. Huge, thick, termite nests perch high up in the trees. Occasionally a darting lizard emerges from the thicket onto the path and then quickly skitters away into nearby foliage. Everywhere there is lush greenery, tropical flowers, and vivid blue sky peaking between the trees as the branches gently sway in the breeze.

Anne and Patrick are already at the beach having planted themselves under shady palm trees for yet another relaxing day.

I imagine that they have strolled the beach, bodysurfed gentle ocean waves, and are now relaxing in the loveliness around them. Patrick will likely be sprawled out on a blanket engrossed in one of several novels he will consume this week. Anne will be deep in concentration, creating paintings with water from the ocean and her trusty tray of watercolor paints. Small pieces of art will manifest one after the next on thick bumpy paper, pastels blending into miniature abstract paintings.

My Friend Irene

As I walk down the path, I turn inward and am deep in thought about my friend Irene who died suddenly of Stage IV cancer, just twelve months ago, a quick and painful three weeks from diagnosis to passing. I miss her terribly and wish she were here, strolling down to the beach with me. I feel that familiar sinking sensation in the pit of my stomach when I remember she is gone. Life is emptier now without the light and fun she brought to almost everything.

Our twenty-year friendship started when we were coworkers and blossomed into travel buddies, co-conspirators, and confidantes. I think about the many hot summer afternoons floating in the nearly empty swimming pool at her condominium—a lovely, quiet place surrounded by lush green trees with plenty of room to spread out and relax. We would spend hours analyzing politics and voicing our viewpoints. We chatted about Hollywood celebrities, famous entertainers, and royalty. Occasionally we talked about work but mostly we shared our deep love for movies and travel.

During her last few years, we had traveled together to England, Scotland, and Spain. We took winter getaways with our daughters to the sandy beaches of Mexico and laughed our way through many out-of-town girls' weekends. We could always find a cause for celebration: milestones birthdays, graduations, and much-needed breaks from routine life. We consoled each other during the rough patches in each of our lives, celebrated our victories, and advised each other about the important things constantly—welcome or not.

I still cannot make sense of her death.

During the final weeks of her life, I lived in a constant state of dread, on edge, and on the verge of tears. I spent long days with her when she was in the hospital and then hospice, trailing along with her daughter from appointment to appointment, doing whatever I could to be helpful and remain upbeat. But despite exceptional care and the most positive disposition I could muster, she died anyway.

And then an amazing thing happened.

After she died a little over a year ago, my life changed suddenly in the most startling and unlikely way. I began to feel her presence around me.

During the first few months following Irene's passing, I would catch sudden glimpses of her out of the corner of my eye. Every few days I would *see* her with her long, beautiful auburn hair—she would be crossing a room, standing in a crowd, sitting in the passenger seat of my car. She was a vision in my mind that appeared so real I believed if I reached out, I could touch her.

One night in March, three months after her funeral, I had the first of many lucid dreams that occurred every few weeks throughout the first year of her passing. In each dream, I joyfully reconnected with her, and her messages came in symbols and signs to support what she was communicating for me to pass along to her daughter and others. So sudden and intense were the dreams that I hastily recorded their details in a journal by my bedside before they faded away, often in the middle of the night.

The dreams were filled with imagery and nuance, and I captured the essence of the messages she was conveying to me without stopping to determine their meaning. I communicated with Irene about her death and what she was experiencing in her new life, and she passed along wisdom for living in this world. I would ask her in these dreams if she knew she was dead and she would quickly reply, "Of course!" in her easygoing, matter-of-fact way.

Around the time that I was experiencing the lucid dreams, I began to communicate with Irene through journaled conversations. Every few days I would notice a distinct tingling sensation on the top of my head that would catch me off guard. Instantly I would sense her presence surrounding me and I would intuitively know that she wanted to communicate with me. I would grab my journal, find a place to sit quietly, and close my eyes to block out distractions. Then I would rapidly record her conversation with me for the twenty minutes or so that she was present.

Throughout the first year following Irene's death, I filled several journals with dreams and scrawled messages. Over time I found comfort reading through the passages that were consistently filled

Lush jungles of Costa Rica

with love and messages of hope to those of us she left behind. In one reading she told me she was my "pen pal from the other side." In another, that I was her "scribe on earth."

In a journaling session just a week before leaving for Costa Rica, Irene told me she would be coming with me on this journey. "A few others are also coming along." She instructed, "Look for me down by the ocean."

Spinning Leaves

I am thinking about all this as I continue walking the steep path past the yoga studio, the huts, and the large tent. The tropical sun beats down on me. Soon I am walking alongside a long row of vibrant green plants that line the path to my left. Their variegated leaves remind me of *Hosta* foliage. The plants stand side by side for fifteen to twenty yards down the hill, just off the graveled path. The mildest breeze gently ruffles some of the leaves as it passes through the forest.

Suddenly, my eyes are drawn to a specific plant. One leaf is sticking straight up from the base, spinning wildly first to the right, and then to the left! Irrationally, I think that a small animal must be frantically rubbing the stem back and forth with its tiny hands at the base of the plant to get the plant leaf to spin. But of course, there is no small animal.

My jaw drops in amazement. Did I just imagine I saw that? Was the lone leaf really spinning?

In silence I reach out to Irene: "Irene, are you here? Are you trying to get my attention?"

Time stands still. I take in this remarkable experience and I am both delighted and deeply shaken. What has just happened? Am I losing my mind?

After several long moments of contemplation, I continue my journey down to the ocean deep in thought about this startling event.

When I arrive on the private resort beach, Anne and Patrick are the only ones around. Far down the shore, bodysurfers are jumping in the waves, but mostly it is quiet and serene. I see Patrick lounging on a blanket under a shady tree on the edge of the sandy beach, working his way through his third or fourth book. He is fully absorbed in his reading.

A short distance away, Anne is sitting on a blanket. She is engrossed in painting abstract images that are smaller than a postcard. These are soul paintings—a term she learned years ago while attending a community education Soul Painting for Beginners Class. She tells me she *failed* this class, choosing to ignore directions and create whatever she desired, depending on what she was feeling. Sometimes Anne laughs as she recalls her encouraging parents wondering why she does not paint what already exists. According to Anne, "If I had to paint a banana, I'd never be able to do it!"

The soul paintings are a gift from her heart, and she frequently inserts them into tiny frames and passes them along as thank-you gifts to friends and colleagues. She did, in fact, give several of them to Irene as a thank-you for fresh homemade muffins that Irene would bring to work for Anne and other coworkers.

Anne, Irene, and I were friends and colleagues for many years, working as career coaches with executives and professionals in job transition. As a social media expert, Anne taught classes every Wednesday and would stop in to see Irene—secretly hoping for fresh baked goods. She would find her tiny framed art proudly displayed on bookshelves throughout Irene's office.

Now at the beach, I quickly slip out of my flip flops and bolt across the sand toward Anne. I desperately need to debrief what has just happened. Anne and I share a deep interest in the mystical, spiritual world, the world beyond what we experience through our five senses. In the past year, we have spent countless hours talking through and analyzing the mysterious dreams and journaling experiences I have had with Irene.

I am anxious to tell Anne what has just happened.

"You just won't believe it!" I say, on high alert from what I just experienced. "I think Irene was trying to get my attention by making a plant leaf stand straight up and spin wildly one way and then the other!"

Anne perks up as I continue.

"When I was journaling with her, she told me she was coming to Costa Rica and that I should look for her down at the beach. I think it was her."

Patrick lounging on the beach

"Journal about it," says Anne, "and look for more signs!"

She, too, is on the lookout for inspiration from our friend. I can tell Anne everything I see and experience about Irene. She always encourages me to look deeper at what has happened and to try to make sense of it. Anne is open and attentive to what I share, and she believes deeply, as do I, in synchronicity and signs from loved ones who have passed. We share an insatiable desire to know more—to search deeply and discover the truth about what happens to us when we die, how we can continue our connection with those in the spirit world, and how that can inform us on how to live our best lives.

A Second Sighting

Late the following afternoon, our group gathers for our last class in the yoga studio prior to heading to the beach to practice mild yoga and watch the setting sun. We are sitting cross-legged in a circle on the smooth wood floor, sharing insights about what we have learned throughout the week. Over seven days together many of us have become friends, supporting each other during class and hanging out by the pool and ocean, sharing stories of our lives.

Suddenly a few of the overhead lights blink, then they all go off for a moment ... one, two, three ... and then come back on. Anne and I quickly glance at each other as the startled group reacts with nervous laughter. We have not experienced lights going out at any other time this week. There are mumblings about whether this might be spiritual visitors in this yoga room, and I silently ask, "Irene, are you here? Do you have messages for us? Or is this just my active imagination?"

Ten minutes later, we slowly saunter down to the beach in small groups of two or three for our barefoot yoga session at the water's edge. The sun is gradually descending when we arrive, but it will take a good hour or so until sunset. We settle haphazardly into three rows lined up along the shore and begin morphing our bodies into modified yoga poses. I am so relaxed and, as I breathe in the ocean air deeply, I am filled with joy for the moist sand under my feet and my ability to stretch just a little more than I was able to do earlier in the week. I am beginning to get the hang of this, and I contemplate taking a yoga class when I am back home.

When our yoga session ends, we gather into small groups once again. Almost everyone is jumping in the ocean waves or chatting with one another while we wait for the sun to set. I strike up conversations with new yoga friends, commiserate about how I don't feel that I have progressed much this week, but acknowledge how grateful I am to be here.

Gradually I feel a yearning to separate from the group and walk alone down the beach to the south. It is tropical here, so the beach is different from the pristine sandy beaches I am familiar with along coastal Mexico. This is an uneven shoreline. Tree ruts occasionally poke through the sand, and there is plenty of driftwood, crushed shells, and pebbles. If I stand with bare feet and carefully inspect the sand, I notice that there is an ever-so-slight movement happening as small water bugs dart quickly about, forming intricate geographic patterns in the sand. Along the jungle side of the beach, palm trees, overgrown foliage, and willowy trees bend slightly toward the ocean.

I am about fifteen minutes into my walk, enjoying cool sand on bare feet, when I come upon four short palm trees, perhaps twenty feet high, side by side, their large palm leaves gently arching toward the ground. I am walking past them when suddenly I notice something shocking out of the corner of my eye! There is only an occasional light breeze that moves a palm leaf or two, but now one leaf—just one—rises to tower over the other leaves and is frantically bending back and forth, twisting, and turning. I am astonished. This is mimicking the plant from my walk to the beach yesterday. Now I know Irene is here! She told me she will see me at the beach. I have my proof!

I want to turn around and shout "Come quickly and see this!" to the others who are out of earshot, so they can witness what I am seeing. I want them to verify that they, too, see the twisting palm leaf frantically waving its message. But I remain silent. Who will believe my story? Will they see what I see? Have I made this all up?

Sunset at Blue Spirit Resort

It is time for me to venture back now. The sun is setting, and it will be a dark walk through the jungle. I am deeply moved, and I quickly carve a message in the moist sand and snap a photo as a memento of what I have experienced.

Message in the sand

Happy Trees

Chapter 2

The Story Begins

A Birthday Gathering

It is late Sunday morning in early November, fourteen months before the yoga retreat in Costa Rica. The air is crisp and there is an icy blue sky and a brisk wind that scatters the remnants of fall across sidewalks and streets. A hint of a chill in the air forewarns of the long, cold winter months to come. Irene and I are celebrating her daughter Sarah's thirty-third birthday with brunch at Sammy's, a quirky neighborhood restaurant and bar on the south side of the city.

I am frequently invited to special family events like this. Irene and I each have just one child, beautiful daughters who are close in age. We love to spend time with them and their friends whenever they allow us to join them.

Sarah is seated across the table, surrounded by best buddies and coworkers who have joined the party. With gorgeous auburn hair like her mother's, and piercing aquamarine eyes, it is not surprising that she was a child model who grew into a mature, confident woman. With her big heart and engaging smile, Sarah has found her calling in life working with inner-city kids as the director of a city park. She is compassionate, courageous, and loves to laugh at the antics of her coworkers and the kids they serve.

Everyone is cheerfully toasting Sarah. The girls banter and laugh about crazy events from the evening before, content that it has been a great weekend so far. Irene, the host of this party, is bright and upbeat—always one to make sure everyone has a great time. As a single mom, she raised Sarah alone from the time she was five, and it is Irene's mission in life to surround Sarah with never-ending love and support. As Sarah and her friends acknowledge, Irene has a heart of gold.

Gazing on this joyful scene unfolding, I think about how Irene has been telling me over the past few weeks that she's been feeling "a bit off." Headaches come and go, and she is tired. She missed a few days of work and hopes to feel better soon.

I turn to her and softly ask "How are you feeling today?" and, with a weary voice, she leans in and quietly says "Not great." Instantly, she turns back to smile at the girls and join in the fun.

A week later I call Irene to see if she is feeling any better. Though it is Monday, she tells me, "I probably won't be going to work for the rest of the week."

I think to myself—who does that? Who knows on Monday that they will be sick the entire week? It doesn't sound good to me. I feel the first small twinge of worry that something might be seriously wrong with my optimistic friend who always assumes the best.

Memories of Spain

My mind drifts back to memories of Spain from the trip we took together just a month earlier. I recall the empty bottle of a hundred Advil tablets that she consumed over ten days because her hip was sore, and she had frequent headaches and fatigue. Now I wonder if her current illness is related to these symptoms.

As travel buddies, we had booked a fall tour to Spain and added in extra days for traveling on our own. We were excited to explore Barcelona, Madrid, and Toledo with a tour group, and then travel to Seville by train, and fly back to Barcelona for the end of our journey. We knew that we would have the best time possible if someone else arranged hotels, tours, and other travel plans so we could focus on having fun and enjoying new friendships.

Barcelona

Spain was everything we had hoped for, and more. We followed an invigorating daily schedule with early morning breakfasts of cheeses, cold cuts, thick grainy breads, cappuccinos, and lattes. Brisk walks to tour historic museums and breathtaking cathedrals rich with history. We strolled down the cobbled streets of the old towns, poking in and out of quaint shops filled with voices bantering in their beautiful Spanish language. Exhausted, we would take a quick siesta back at our hotel, then head out once again for dinner and drinks at lively restaurants tucked away in neighborhoods just off the beaten path of the inner city.

Toledo

On the first evening of our tour, we mingled with our new tour friends over dinner at a small restaurant in a quiet neighborhood in the northern edge of Barcelona. We had started with a two-mile walk through the crowded, lively streets of old town, our guide pointing out some of the unusual and one-of-a-kind buildings designed by world-renowned Spanish architect Antoni Gaudi. Then, came a fifteen-minute train ride followed by more walking down several zig-zagging side streets until we arrived at our destination. It had taken nearly an hour to arrive and we were famished. Spirits were high as wine poured freely and we were soon savoring our first exquisite Spanish dinner.

In the restaurant, closed to the public for our boisterous eighteen-member group, we were packed tightly into a cluster of long tables. First wine, then appetizers, dinner, dessert, more wine. Irene and I sat across from two fellow travelers and, as we dined, I asked them, "What made you decide to travel with a tour group to Spain?"

A long pause later, Andrea, a forty-something woman with beautiful red hair, leaned forward, wine glass in hand, as if to engage us in an intimate conversation. In a whispering voice, she said, "I have Stage IV lung cancer and I wasn't going to tell anyone. I just finished chemotherapy and I made a commitment to myself that I was going to take this trip to Spain, no matter what!" She added, "I've never smoked in my life and I am still in shock and so angry that I have cancer."

We were stunned and in awe. Quickly glancing at one another, we murmured our approval of her courageous move and raised our glasses to toast our new friend. She looked so healthy and happy. How was it possible that she could be dealing with the aftermath of cruel cancer treatments and the emotional roller coaster of such a devastating illness? We gushed over her bravery and committed to helping her with anything she needed in the days ahead.

As the week unfolded, first in Barcelona and then Madrid, we had many opportunities to spend time with Andrea. One night after a long day of touring, Irene told me that Andrea was her favorite new acquaintance on the tour saying, "I don't know; there's just something about her I really like."

I thought it might have something to do with both being natural redheads with lively personalities. I believe now that theirs was a connection on a much deeper soul level.

On the final evening of our tour, we once again sat across from Andrea and her husband Bill in a festive Spanish restaurant in old-town Madrid. Over Spanish cabernet and rich, delicate tapas, we talked about the sights we had seen, places we had visited, and the open market in the town square. Earlier that day, Irene had negotiated the purchase of a stunning scarf of rich brown, cream, and rust colors from a fast-talking street vendor. She now had it draped gracefully across her shoulders.

Andrea admired the scarf and commented, "My daughter would just *love* the colorful design of that scarf! It would look so beautiful against her complexion." Without a second thought, Irene removed the scarf and gently handed it to her amazed friend Andrea as a parting gift to pass along to her daughter.

As I witnessed this selfless and generous act, I realized that I had always admired my friend's giving heart and compassion for so many others. Pure, unconditional love.

Heartbreaking Diagnosis

November is a terrible month. Irene has been to way too many doctors' appointments, has had numerous tests and body scans—even a brain scan—and continues to feel worse.

As the days go by, she is finally feeling so weak that she calls Sarah to drive her to the hospital on the Friday before Thanksgiving as she is to meet with an oncologist to discuss lab results. By now Irene is so sick she tells Sarah that after meeting with the oncologist she will insist on being admitted to the hospital until they find out what is wrong with her.

On Friday morning, I am with Irene, Sarah, and Irene's cousin as the oncologist quietly shares the Stage IV lung cancer diagnosis with Irene. The news is devastating and impossible to comprehend. How can she have lung cancer when she never smoked a day in her life? I feel emotional pain—like being punched in the stomach. Sarah is keeping up a strong front, but I know that she is deeply shocked as the news sinks in.

Now we must focus on all available solutions because it is not in our realm of possibility that Irene won't beat this cancer. We are going to do everything we can to make sure she gets well. We have an unspoken pact that we will keep positive for Irene. Only when she is out of proximity will we share our deepest fears.

The oncologist clearly understands the gravity of the diagnosis, but he is helping us cope by considering each of the alternatives we pose: immunotherapy? radiation? chemotherapy? a combination? What would he do if he had such a diagnosis? He replies, "I guess I would want to know if immunotherapy would be a possibility, but more tests will need to be done." He assures us that additional tests will evaluate the extent of the cancer and determine treatment options.

For the rest of this emotionally exhausting day, we move underground from one unit of the hospital to another through long institutional corridors, scuffed grey floors and white walls. At a meeting in the radiology department, more treatment options are apprehensively suggested by a radiologist who has seen too much and knows the odds. Irene is clearly physically and mentally exhausted, and by mid-afternoon, she is finally admitted to the hospital.

Saturday morning brings a parade of cheerful, friendly caregivers floating in and out of Irene's hospital room to talk about support services. "Would you like aromatherapy? We can give you a massage if you'd like."

Irene is game for all of it. There are nurses attending to blood pressure, temperature, and other vital signs. Soft shoes and compassionate hearts.

Throughout the weekend Sarah and I make sure that Irene is never alone. Friends, relatives, and colleagues all come for short visits and there are laughs and tears between the somber moments. Irene perks up as each guest arrives, always one to love parties and festivities of any kind. She wants to know, "How are things at work? Weren't you just out of town? Tell me about it."

Anne stops by when she can to provide support and encouragement, trying her best to make everything right once again.

Though these are serious times, all of us, including Irene, try to keep the conversation light. We laugh over funny stories; reminisce about good times we've had together. Surely if we surround Irene with enough of our positivity and healing prayers, she will return to good health. Only when she dozes off once again do we gather in the hallways or the lounge. Our hushed conversations are filled with concern and helplessness. Everyone is hoping for a miracle.

A Thanksgiving Break

The following Tuesday Irene broaches the idea of going home for Thanksgiving, her favorite holiday. She absolutely *must* be home to prepare her annual feast for family and friends that rivals five-star dining. Cooking begins days before the event, tables are set with the best china and crystal along with colorful fall floral arrangements and customized place cards. She is worried about Thanksgiving preparations even while she is lying in a hospital bed. Thanksgiving must go on.

Nurses come in and out of the room to take blood pressure and tend to charts. When she mentions Thanksgiving, they say, "We'll see" in a noncommittal voice. In the meantime, Sarah and her friend Shannon have already decided to host Thanksgiving at Irene's condo. They promise to tidy the place up and order a full meal for twenty from a local upscale grocer.

"You can rest while we set tables, prepare and serve the meal, and get everyone to help clean up."

This is not the way Irene would have it, but it will have to do this year.

As it turns out, Irene does get released to go home for Thanksgiving with stern instructions that she must come back if her health gets worse. Later, I hear from her family that she was too tired to participate in much of the activity and spent most of her time reclined on her white leather couch under a thick woolly blanket, watching the festivities. I am sure there is nowhere on earth she would rather have been, but I imagine that as the day wore on, she became more and more exhausted from the activities and the guests she loves so much.

She is aware that final test results are in and treatment options are being considered. She will return to the hospital for an appointment early next week to discuss what will happen next.

A Mystical Memory

Sarah is on family leave from work and has temporarily moved into her mom's condominium to take care of her mom as best she can. Irene's parents died years ago and her siblings live across the country, so local relatives and friends cover caretaking in shifts, assuring someone is with Irene 24-7. No one knows if she has any options to fight this cancer, but we will keep her comfortable and do what we can.

Saturday afternoon, two days after Thanksgiving, I am alone in Irene's condo for my shift. Sarah has gone to run errands and Irene is asleep in her bedroom with the door closed. It is eerily quiet. This no longer feels like the bright, cheerful place I know and love. Stillness cascades from the skylights and covers everything.

I want to talk with Irene and see if there is anything she needs, but more than anything I want to have a *real* conversation with her, like the ones we've had for the past twenty years. I want to banter about the elections, hear what she's been up to, laugh about some silly thing happening out in Hollywood. I am so hoping there will still be time for those conversations. I sit quietly on the big leather couch. Time slowly ticks by. I can't concentrate on the book I brought to read.

As I look around her spacious light-filled condo, I can't help but think back to all the celebrations that have occurred here, including a year ago when Irene hosted a champagne brunch for my birthday. One day, late in August, we were floating on colorful Styrofoam noodles in her swimming pool when she suddenly turned to me and said, with a twinkle in her eyes, "I think you need a birthday party and I want to host it! Just give me a list of who you want there and I'll make all the plans."

I could see her losing herself in the pure joy of planning the party, smiling as she floated in the pool: lists to be created; decorations and a color scheme to choose, a menu to perfect, an amazing cake that she would serve.

On a gorgeous Sunday afternoon, a month later, I was the guest of honor at a delightful and memorable birthday brunch. Fancy china, flutes of champagne, fresh-cut flowers, laughter filling the air. Light streamed into the living room from overhead skylights and through the sliding glass doors that open onto a grassy hillside. During brunch, we sat in the dining room, an interior room with no windows or skylight, which opens to the living room. The champagne flowed as we ate and talked and laughed, old and new friends connecting.

After several toasts, cell phones were retrieved from purses and photos were taken one after another to capture the moments. My cell phone was at the far end of the table nearest the living room. Irene and I were surrounded by guests at the opposite end of the dining room where the only light shining on us came from the overhead chandelier. Four photos were taken in quick succession before my phone was set down on the table once again.

As I reviewed the photos later that afternoon, I was shocked to see that the lighting in three photos was the same, but the fourth photo showed a darkened room with a huge beam of light cascading down upon me and Irene. Another faint beam reached out toward Anne who sat off to the side of us.

Dining room – photo one

Dining room – photo two

I was stunned. This was no fluke, no lighting mishap. The beam that enveloped us in the surrounding darkness looked like golden light coming from the heavens to bless us. I have heard that angels and spiritual beings are sometimes captured on photographs and I wondered if this is what had appeared.

For weeks I showed this photo to anyone willing to look at it. The reaction was instantaneous: "Wow! What is that? I've never seen anything like it." Some suggested that I had captured spirit in the photo and that this was indeed a blessing being bestowed upon us.

As I sit here now, all these months later, I still think of that photo and the meaning behind it. What a blessing to be in the light with her, but why did that happen? What does it mean?

I bring myself back to the present moment, sitting in Irene's condo, realizing I have been lost in this memory for some time. It is getting dark outside now and Sarah will be home soon. When we have a changing of the guards, I walk out into the cold evening, comforted that Sarah will be there to care for her sweet mom.

From Hospital to Hospice

Early Monday morning, Irene is re-admitted to the hospital. The past few days have brought a serious decline in her health and, even though Sarah has been a pillar of strength for weeks on end, it is no longer possible for her to care for her mom at home.

Final test results are in. The gentle oncologist helps Irene understand that neither immunotherapy nor chemotherapy will be helpful now. It is time to consider hospice options.

Out-of-state relatives arrive, grateful to be spending whatever time they can with Irene. When she is awake and coherent, she is all business. Propped up in the hospital bed, she works on financial and legal issues that she wants to resolve for Sarah. An attorney comes to help her with her will. She is the industrious Irene I know, attending to the necessary details. The spurts of energy are in stark contrast to her declining health.

Sarah and I, along with some close friends and relatives, help Irene settle into the hospice home that she has chosen for her final care. Though we do not know what to expect, this is a hospice home filled with warmth and kindness. Tucked discretely into a quiet tree-lined neighborhood, the large hospice home has room for many patients and large comfortable living areas to accommodate visitors. In the living room outside Irene's room, we settle into overstuffed couches and chairs speaking quietly and monitoring a steady stream of visitors to make sure they are not overtaxing Irene by staying too long and absorbing too much of her energy. There are large Christmas trees and plenty of spirited, festive lights throughout the hospice home. Overall, it is a pleasant place.

Irene's room is homey and comforting and she lies in bed in pajamas that are made of the same tiny pink rose pattern as the sheets. I know that if she were more alert, she would be exclaiming about all the great touches for people staying there. The smell of cookies baking fills the air. There is even a fireplace in her bedroom, and this is as close to home as you can get for a healthcare setting.

The frantic activities of working through the medical system over the past few weeks have come to a halt. There is no more possibility for a miraculous cure … no chance for a life extension.

From time to time I sit in a chair by her bedside and softly talk with her as she fades in and out of a deep sleep that seems to take her somewhere far away. I tell her, "Irene, I'm so sorry that you're here. This is just unbelievable. I'll be here for the long haul—I'm not going anywhere. I promise to watch over Sarah—she's going to be okay."

Irene glances up at me as though she wants to smile or nod, but she is so weak and quickly falls back asleep. When she does speak to me, I cannot understand what she is saying.

Though her health is deteriorating rapidly, and she never leaves her bed, in the final days there are moments of lightness. One day I am sitting by her bedside while she is dozing, when she suddenly opens her eyes, looks at me, and with great clarity says, "Well, I don't even know what to say about this!" then promptly falls back to sleep.

Another time a baby is crying in the living room outside her room and Irene's eyes fly open. In distress she says, "There's a baby crying … is the baby alright?" And then quickly collapses back into a deep sleep.

Once she wakes abruptly. "Did Kim Kardashian have her baby? Is it a boy or a girl?" she asks, before drifting away once more.

One day a music therapist comes to visit; another day brings out-of-town relatives who will stay for the duration. Family friends with babies come calling. Coworkers come and go.

Anne visits daily and once quietly says to Irene, "Please send us signs," to which Irene mutters, "I'm not dead yet!" Another day, Anne again asks Irene to send signs and she quips, "I don't believe in that!"

A few days earlier, in a moment lacking clarity, several of us decide it would be fun for some family members and friends to rent a limo and take Irene out of hospice on Sunday evening to see Christmas lights around the city. As the time nears, we realize there is not a chance this is going to happen—Irene is not going to leave hospice and she knows it even if we don't. Irene, being clear-headed when we are not, insists "Go and have fun. I'll be fine resting here." Sarah will stay behind to be with her.

When the limo arrives, the rest of us pile in and we find the ride therapeutic and lovely. In normal times, Irene would be beyond excited for this adventure, but these are not normal times and we are all going at her insistence. Though there is sharing and laughter in the limo, and the lights are beautiful, it is a somber event. We know we do not have much time left with our dear friend, and we are already beginning to process the grief that will be our constant companion for months to come.

Going Home

Tuesday, December 15 is a clear, cold winter day. I am planning to visit Irene after client meetings. As a career coach, I have appointments and calls to make before my planned early afternoon arrival at the hospice home.

A client I had a coaching session with on Monday has left me a curt phone message that she would like to talk to me at 2:00 p.m. today. There is a cold tone to her voice that takes me by surprise. We had a productive meeting just yesterday, and she told me upon parting that she was looking forward to our next session.

Though I had planned to be at hospice by 2:00 p.m., I call my client by phone instead and am taken totally off guard when she tells me, "I am extremely disappointed in the work we are doing together. I don't know if I want to continue to work with you." She doesn't give me any clear reason why things aren't working. I am shocked. This seems to be coming out of left field. I know that the session went well, and this does not align at all with my experience of working with her.

Quickly, I try to understand what has happened and wonder how I can resolve the situation. I am getting nowhere in understanding what has upset her. She becomes more and more agitated and it is 2:45 p.m. before I finally end the call with my still-dissatisfied client. I bolt out the door on my way to the hospice home. Time is so precious now and I want to spend all the time that I can with my friend.

I arrive at 3:00 p.m. and rush into Irene's bedroom. I know the moment I walk in that she is gone. As quickly as grief comes over me, I also feel deep anger and resentment. How could I allow myself to get sucked into such a long conversation with a disgruntled client who was strange right from the start? How could I possibly have missed being here with Sarah when Irene passed?

I cannot let go of the rage I feel about the client who got in my way until Anne suggests later that perhaps there is a Divine plan. Could it be that it was important that I NOT be there in the end? What if it was Irene's last desire to be alone with her daughter and her cousin when she took her last breath? As I slowly take in Anne's words, they ring true for me and I see that the annoying client was merely playing her part in a larger life drama.

Afternoon turns to evening. The sun has faded, and we are gathered in the living room, greeting final guests, sharing tears and memories. Finally, it is time to leave the cocoon we have been in for the past five days to attend to what comes next. As I walk out into the cold night, I feel deep sadness and dread for the grief that is to come.

Goodnight, Irene

YEAR ONE

After Life

Chapter 3

Glimpses of Irene in Winter

Giving a Eulogy

There is much to be done now—a eulogy to write, the funeral, burial, Shiva—the days of planning go by quickly. A few relatives, a colleague, and I are giving eulogies, and then after a few words from the rabbi, we will be off to the burial site.

I write my eulogy in starts and stops. How difficult to put into a few short words twenty years of friendship and all the good times we shared. Through my words, I want to bring Irene alive—to speak of her heart and compassion and delightful humor. I want to illustrate these words with endearing stories. The rabbi says, "Five minutes tops, per eulogy," so I know I need to be succinct.

The morning of the funeral is bitterly cold with a brilliant blue sky. As we gather in a back room with the rabbi before the service begins, I am struck by what a privilege it is to be in this inner circle of extended family and friends that surround the large conference table, solemn and quieted. I am a jumble of emotions, both nervous and calm. I am honored that I will hold a torch high for my friend and I still cannot believe that this is happening. The rabbi offers some comfort, says a few prayers, and then we are ready for the event.

We are in a lovely, peaceful synagogue. Light streams through towering overhead windows onto the benches forming a semicircle in front of the altar. Guests occupy the benches in the center and to the left, and there are a few empty rows of seating in front on the right. With notes clenched in hand, I approach the podium with a silent inner command to maintain my calmness: No crying! Don't waste this precious opportunity to honor your friend by being nervous or self-absorbed!

I stand at the podium knowing that this is what it feels like to be grown up—to give a eulogy for my friend, for the sake of love, setting all fears and inhibitions aside. If I cry—so be it.

As soon as I begin sharing stories of Irene, I instantly feel at home with this group of friends and family. I scan the congregation as I tell story after story, and see that they are engaged, smiling, nodding, and laughing loudly from time to time. I am speaking of my fondest memories of her when I notice out of the corner of my eye that she is here! I see her clearly in my mind's eye—her long auburn hair catching the beams of sunlight pouring down through the windows. She is sitting on a front-row bench to my right, which gives her a perfect view of the congregation. She is beaming and radiant, healthy, and vibrant, showing no signs of illness. She scans the crowd as though to capture all the love that flows from them.

At first, I feel pure joy. My friend died—but here she is! I see her just as plainly as I have seen her a million times in the past. She is as amused and entertained by the eulogies as many of the members of the congregation are. Yet, there is something going on here that defies logic—I am giving a eulogy about her to her!

Almost immediately I wipe these thoughts from my mind. It's so wonderful to think that she is here, but I need to get a grip. She has passed on and it is likely I am still in denial. On the other hand, it would be so like her to want to join in the festivities—the ultimate social butterfly!

I speak of our friendships: the travels we took, our passion for movies and politics, the career we shared. I tell a quick story from Spain: "One day in Madrid, we were on a tour of parliament. Sometimes the tour guides would get long-winded and Irene would turn to me in exasperation and quietly whisper, 'They just go on and on and on!'

"About half-way through the tour, we entered a ballroom where a huge gilded portrait of the Spanish royal family was centered prominently on the north wall. Then the tour guide said the magic words, 'There has been a great deal of scandal in the royal family recently,' and as the group paused to let that sink in, Irene snapped to attention and moved right to the front of the line with question after question." She was always a royal watcher.

Then I add in a story from our trip to England and one from Mexico, telling them, "We arrived in London a few years ago after an all-night flight. We were exhausted and in dire need of a quick nap. But, it turned out that our hotel was near Buckingham Palace and, when Irene realized that, we had to immediately take a brisk two-mile walk over to tour Princess Diana's apartment and see if the current guards had ever met her. She also got the scoop on whether they knew Prince William and the Duchess of Cambridge, Kate Middleton, and tried to find out anything she could about them too, to no avail.

I describe how we traveled a few times to our favorite Mexican getaway in Ixtapa. Irene would research in advance to find out which celebrities had been sighted in which restaurants, so we could check those out. She would ask wait staff and cab drivers if they had served those celebrities and if so, she wanted to know what they were like. I always felt like we were just a brush away from fame.

Finally, I speak about the qualities that defined Irene and the life she lived. I was always amazed that she knew everyone from her condominium complex who came down to the swimming pool. "Hi, Irene," they would shout and wave as they walked through the gate. Irene always seemed to know what was going on in their lives and with their families. If she didn't already know them well, she'd strike up a conversation and find common ground.

I tell about how she was patient, kind, and a great listener with friends of all ages. She was a second mom to so many of Sarah's friends. Irene was always the first to suspect celebrity foul play and was on top of all political news. She loved her work—helping people—and bringing out the best in others. She was the 'Queen of Hospitality,' bringing class and style to everything she did. Family, friends, and especially Sarah were the most important people in life to her.

In closing, I tell the audience what I admired most in Irene is that she lived her life with no regrets. She was kind, humble, and grateful for every new day and for her many friendships.

After the eulogies are complete, the rabbi says final prayers and we quickly depart from the synagogue for the cemetery. The burial is in a small Jewish cemetery across town. With a handful of friends and family watching from nearby, Irene's urn of ashes is lowered into the ground. I know I am witnessing a significant event, yet, amazingly, I feel no sadness. I simply do not believe she is in that urn and, though the words from the rabbi are spoken with grace and reverence, it feels like nothing more than ritual. I know that once she passed away, her expansive, loving spirit left her body that could no longer contain it. For the first time in my life, I truly know that we do not die, and that death is merely a brief transition from one kind of life to another.

Shiva has begun and days later Sarah, some girlfriends, and relatives host a lovely gathering for Irene. It's the Saturday night before Christmas and yet this calm and loving gathering is in sharp contrast to the last-minute frenetic busyness of the holidays in the outside world. There are personal touches of Irene every-where, from her favorite foods to *People*, *Vanity Fair*, and *Entertain-ment Weekly* magazines on every table. Sarah has made sure that this event honoring her mom is of the caliber that her mom would host. Everyone can see that it is.

Most of the guests are still dazed about her quick passing, and there is also a radiating warmth among the tears as people fondly tell stories and share memories about the many sides of Irene.

A photograph of Irene is prominently on display among beau-tiful bouquets of flowers, and there are framed copies for Sarah and Irene's closest friends and relatives. Just two months earlier, when we were in the world-famous *Sagrada Familia* cathedral in Barcelona, a tour guide had been extolling the important features of the cathedral for over an hour. Irene would occasionally drift away to look at something that caught her eye. Raised in the Jew-ish faith, she would comment from time to time, "I've seen enough of the cathedrals!"

Suddenly she stopped and asked me if I would take a pic-ture of her standing by one of the pillars in the sanctuary. She wanted it for the grandson of a good friend. So, as the morning sun was streaming through magnificent stained-glass windows, I snapped the photo as she smiled directly into the camera and waved.

For just a split second I felt the reverence of this moment. Now I wonder if she may have already had a sense that she would be leaving us soon and wanted to leave us with a loving goodbye.

January Visits

With a new year beginning, life slows to a crawl. Cold, bleak Janu-ary has settled in and there is no reprieve. Frigid night creeps in through frosted windowpanes. I constantly yearn to crawl under my covers and sleep the months away. I despise grief, yet there is no way around it. It weighs me down and makes my heart and body ache.

Life has changed dramatically. We gather as friends and colleagues to console one another and share happier times, but everyone is still in shock. When we meet for after-work happy hour, no one is happy. There is no escaping the reality that Irene is no longer with us.

We miss Irene's lively, lighthearted presence and her amusing stories about life at her condo. Her condominium complex, consisting of two buildings housing mostly single residents and older couples, was tucked neatly into a quiet suburban neighborhood with plenty of open space, big trees, and rolling hills. "What's going on at the condo *now*?" we'd ask as we settled in for yet another hilarious story. She kept us entertained for years with tales of the silly antics of the characters living there and of the condo association committee of which she was a popular and active member.

Irene loved condo living and, not long after moving in, she became a member of the condo association. "I need to know what's going on!" she said, looking disapprovingly at the outdated lobby décor and the closed-off swimming pool. Within weeks she got permission and funds to revamp the interior decorating in her three-story building, replacing tired silk-flower arrangements and last-century knickknacks with updated art in bold colors, and bringing in contemporary furnishings.

Then she attacked the outdoor swimming pool area with gusto, replacing deck furniture and adding huge potted geraniums to complement the splashy table umbrellas. The pool area, a private vista surrounded by huge gorgeous trees, was her personal terrain and we spent many weekend afternoons in that nearly empty swimming pool, basking in the warm sunshine.

Condo pool

Awards Season

Awards season is upon us and nominees are announced for the Academy Awards, Golden Globes, Screen Actors Guild Awards, and others. I miss my movie buddy and critic who is no longer here to keep me abreast of up-to-the-minute movie ratings and the latest Hollywood news.

Often, on early Saturday mornings throughout late fall and early winter, my phone would ring, jarring me out of a sound sleep. Before answering, I would already know who was on the other end. Then I would hear Irene's enthusiastic voice. "Well, I've read all the reviews in *Vanity Fair*, *Entertainment Weekly*, and *People*, and I think it's down to three movies we *have* to see … two new releases and a foreign film."

Like clockwork, I would reply, "Irene—it's so early!"

But she would not be dissuaded. Right then, we would make weekend plans for the movies we "had to see!" We frantically tried to fit in as many movies as possible to make certain we were prepared for all the award ceremonies.

Award days were major events and Irene would "make a day of it," settling in to watch privately, assuring no one was talking or distracting her during the important parts. She would call me during the commercial breaks. "Can you *believe* it! No way! He didn't deserve 'supporting actor'—he was horrible!"

I would also be watching with my ballot of potential winners filled out with my best guesses. We would rehash the results at the end of the show and for days and weeks after until it was time to begin the new movie season.

This year, award season will go on without us. I haven't seen a single movie in the past two months.

Something Is Changing

By mid-January, I start to sense Irene's presence nearby; it is startling. I could swear I see the swish of her long auburn hair out of the corner of my eye every few days. I am certain that she is sitting on my living room sofa or standing among a crowd of people nearby. These are fleeting images in my mind, and I think I must be imagining her presence. I question myself relentlessly. "Am I trying to hold on longer?" and "Am I denying the reality that she died?" I remember seeing her in my mind's eye as I was delivering her eulogy at the funeral, but wasn't that just a fluke?

Some days, I am sure that she is sitting in the passenger seat of my car looking out the window while I'm driving. I sense and feel her presence—warm energy radiating from her body and brushing against my arm. I speak to her aloud: "Irene, is that you?" and though I do not hear her reply to me, I imagine that she wants me to know that she is right here, with me. I converse with her in my mind (and sometimes aloud). "Are you really here? Why did you come?" The experiences feel so real that in these moments I believe that Irene's death was just a bad dream and life has returned to normal.

As the weeks go by, I catch glimpses of her more frequently, in hallways, across a crowded lobby. I am beyond excited and I want to shout out to everyone "My friend died but I keep seeing her!" Yet, I know how crazy that sounds to most people. I especially want to share what I am experiencing with Sarah, in hopes that I can provide comfort to her that perhaps her mom is alive and well—just not here physically. It is a delicate balance. We grieve death, yet can't we also have hope that souls live on and we can connect with them?

I don't know when she will appear, but I can speak aloud to her (or silently in my mind), "Irene, where are you? Come and visit!" and she will be around me instantly. We sit together in my living room—me flipping channels from news to mindless sitcoms and back to news. I see her sitting across the room on the comfy gold coach—watching TV along with me, as Tiger, my sleepy orange tabby cat, gazes lazily from time to time in her direction. Though she does not speak to me, she appears at ease and comfortably relaxed.

I want to talk with her—to have her tell me *everything* about what she has gone through in leaving this earth and going on to her new reality. Just as in old times, I want all the details. *Where are you? What do you think of the place? What's it like? What do you do with your time?* We have talked about so many things over the years and I yearn to continue to do so.

She remains silent and appears so peaceful. It might seem that this would be disarming—even scare me to my own death, but I feel none of that. I am so grateful that she is nearby. She casually watches TV with me until her presence eventually fades.

A Reality Check

I speak cautiously about what I am experiencing with close friends and family. Watching for their reaction, I notice the attentive and searching way they look into my eyes—-*Are you telling the truth?* I ask myself, *Do I really believe this is happening? Do they really believe this could be happening?*

I do not want to offend those who believe that once a person dies, they are gone forever. People might think I am irreverent or attention-seeking, yet I am neither of those things. I am simply seeing and sensing the presence of my friend who has passed away and she seems as real as when she was on earth. It is remarkable.

Some people believe that when one passes suddenly, their spirit may not initially realize that they have died and so may not pass immediately to *the other side* (heaven, the universe, the great beyond). The spirit may stay earthbound for a week or two, visiting their loved ones and familiar places before eventually drifting away.

I know that Irene is gone and yet she is also here. She does not seem to be in a rush to go anywhere. I sense she wants me to know that there is just a thin gauzy veil that separates us. She is on the other side of the veil with easy access to stepping back to this side for occasional visits.

I constantly wonder why I am experiencing this, but the answer does not come. I am delighted that Irene is close by, but am I prolonging my own grief? I wonder if anyone else is having these experiences and, if so, why are they not talking about it? And most of all, I wonder when these experiences will fade.

Insights from Numerology

It is late January, a month after Irene's death, when I have my first-ever numerology reading with Wes Hamilton, a Spiritual Life

Leadership Coach, a Master Numerologist, and Vice President of Core Passion. *Numerology*, as defined by Wikipedia, is "the divine or mystical relationship between a number and one or more coinciding events. It is also the study of the numerical value of the letters in words, names, and ideas." To me, it is a big mystery, but I am open to learning more.

For more than twenty years, Wes has been providing numerology readings and interpretations to business leaders and others who want to understand the impact of numerology on their life. He is a spiritual leadership coach and teacher who relies on his well-developed intuition and strong insight to enhance his work with clients, and is an expert in integrating the body, mind, and spirit as essential components for leadership. His wife, Lori Palm, is CEO of Core Passion; an innovative assessment tool that guides people and businesses to discover their unique gifts. Together, Wes and Lori are a dynamic duo in the business of inspiring passion, purpose, and possibility for personal and business success.

Wes helps people understand who they are and what drives them through the ancient practice of numerology. Using a client's personal numerology chart, Wes helps his clients recognize the specific influences and opportunities in their life over days, months, and years. In this way, his clients can understand what they might do to prepare beforehand for challenges and opportunities that may appear in their lives.

Anne had nudged me into scheduling this numerology reading with Wes. Anne and I trust each other's intuitive insights and a few weeks ago she said to me, "It would be great for you to understand your numerology, and Wes is the one you want to see. He's the best!" Once again, I do not know what Anne has gotten me into, but I willingly act on her suggestion.

Wes and I are now sitting across from each other on overstuffed brown leather furniture in the studio he created in the lower level of his home. It is a cozy and calming place, locked away from daily distractions: a low ceiling, soft carpeting, throw pillows, and a door that encloses us. Here I can relax and focus on what he will teach me. It is a very cool place with stunning crystals and small rugged rocks scattered across the glass table in front of me; interesting Native American artifacts and other handcrafted artwork hang on the walls.

A counter area across the room from where I sit has fluorescent lights tucked away under cupboards above the countertop. In the months ahead, I experience these lights flickering from time to time when we are engrossed in conversations that hit on deep levels of truth, as though the spirit world agrees with what we are saying.

I've been looking forward to this experience, yet I am also nervous and on edge about conversing with Wes in case the conversation gets too deep or personal. As a career coach, I am used to asking the questions. I am the one to elicit insights from others and to contemplate the meaning of their answers. I do not have much experience in expressing my deep inner thoughts and feelings to many men in my life, and I am hesitant about how this session will unfold. I do not want to be coaxed into exposing vulnerabilities.

Sitting in his large leather chair, Wes exudes natural warmth and openness mixed in with subtle humor. I am instantly comfortable in his presence. He listens intensely to me throughout our session, from time to time contributing insights and asking thought-provoking questions. "What do you feel about what you are hearing? Does this resonate with you?" I am immensely curious, as well as skeptical, that any combination of numbers can suggest patterns that guide my life. I believe in my own free will, but I concede that there may be some external forces at work guiding my life journey.

As Wes begins to interpret the results in my customized numerology book, I am baffled by the complexity of the process. I want to understand what the numerical patterns say about my life and the path I am on. I want to know what the results can tell me about my life.

Over the next hour, Wes reveals what the numbers say about my Birth Path and my Destiny, as well as how my year is likely to progress month by month. I try to absorb as much as I can (I am thankful that it is being recorded), but there is an overwhelming amount of information to process. He asks questions along the way to elicit my insights and reactions, and slowly I come to realize the kernels of truth that have emerged from the reading.

My personal numerology guide from Wes

My Birth Card, the most significant symbol of who we are in this lifetime, is the Queen of Hearts: an idealist, sociable, loving. As the "Mother of Love," my calling in life includes sharing my love with others—the more the better. The Queen of Hearts resonates with me and I believe this card is reflective of my life.

My Birth Path Number and Destiny Number are both eight (8). Wes says, "This implies that 70 percent of your effort on earth is to bring the spiritual realm into daily living."

My path is about bringing love and spirituality into the work world—a path that fits me like a glove. I am a personal and professional coach who loves to see my clients gain self-understanding and evolve. The combination also suggests a preference for order and structure and achievement in my life. I cringe. I tell Wes "Oh no—that is so boring and sounds so serious!" I prefer to see myself much more as a free spirit: casual, flexible, fun. The numbers seem to tell me otherwise.

A 7 Personal Year Begins

According to numerology, on January 1 of this year I began a 7 Personal Year of the nine-year cycle that will repeat itself throughout my life. Everyone evolves through nine-year cycles throughout their lifetime. The attributes of the year they are in provides guidance for the activities and learnings of that year.

A 7 Personal Year is the time to develop inner powers through meditation, reflection, and contemplation. Wes tells me, "This 7 Personal Year is about taking a deep inner journey throughout the year: read, study spiritual books, go to spiritual retreats, meditate, journal, reflect ... be silent." It is a year when I will spend more time in contemplation than in interacting with the physical world. I sigh loudly. This will be a huge stretch for my highly sociable and industrious self. On the other hand, this might help me to process and reflect on the experiences I am having with Irene following her death.

I am struck by the intensity of this 7 Personal Year and have no idea how I will accomplish deepened spiritual growth. I ask Wes, "What does that even mean? If I follow a deepening path, what will I accomplish? How will I be different because of this?" And most importantly, "How will I *ever* learn to meditate?"

Wes shares with me a Spiritual Leadership Development Practice that he provides, if I am interested. It will help me develop a daily meditation practice to help me go inward and gain more access to my spiritual self and develop my light body. It will be a combination of weekly coaching sessions and twice-daily guided meditations that I will complete at home.

I hesitate briefly, remembering that I am terrible at meditation, my mind constantly chattering and getting off track. But Wes is presenting this option to me and I trust him. I immediately commit to participating in this six- to twelve-month program with Wes Hamilton, Master Numerologist, as my spiritual mentor and guide.

Instinctively I know that this is something I need to do. My life is in turmoil and it is time to peel back the layers of my thoughts and beliefs to see what lies inside me. Irene's sudden death has shaken me to the core. I want to understand her passing from a more spiritual perspective. Is there something to be learned from this? What is happening now that she is no longer here? Why do I keep feeling her presence around me? Am I making this up?

I will attend weekly sessions with Wes to experiment with progressively deeper levels of meditation and will be coached on the impact these meditations are having in my life. From time to time there will be guided imagery exercises within the meditations. A gentle voice will guide me on an internal journey to evoke or generate images in my mind of places or situations. I might find myself walking along a river or recreating a scene from my earlier life. The value of the guided imagery will come from the insights I gain from what my mind creates.

I am to keep a journal of my experiences and any insights that emerge through my daily meditation practice. Once a week for many months, Wes and I will review my notes and try to make sense of what I am learning.

Armed with a new journal in hand, I am ready to begin.

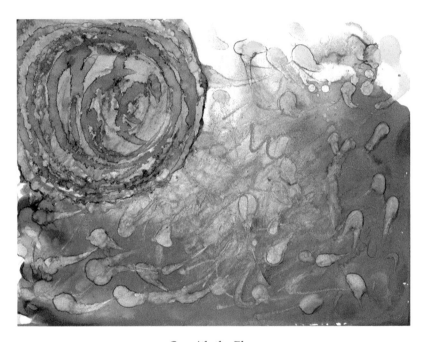

Go with the Flow

Chapter 4

An Inner Journey through Meditation

My First Session with Wes

On a Monday morning in early February, I arrive for my first coaching session with Wes. He greets me at his doorway with a big smile and warm eyes and leads me down the short set of stairs to his studio. I quickly settle in and am ready to let down my guard and talk about anything I want. I am a bundle of emotion: excited and nervous about what I have gotten myself into.

I know that I can always disengage if I get too uncomfortable sharing my thoughts and feelings with Wes. It will not be the first time that I have walked away from something from fear of the unknown or from having to confess to strong emotions. But I know that it is now time to work on authenticity and opening myself to more learning about the mysteries of life and the afterlife. For now, I will stick it out.

Each week, we will reflect on the learnings and experiences from the meditation practice of the previous week, followed by twenty to thirty minutes of meditation that we will experience together. I can ask Wes whatever I want, whenever I want, and I find this immensely satisfying. Where else in my life can I have these in-depth conversations with someone who will challenge me to dig even deeper, with no judgment?

Wes tells me that we will work on developing my spiritual light body from the inside out. I am puzzled; "What does THAT mean?" I ask. I have many spiritual thoughts—but this is different.

Wes says, "This is about quieting your mind and being grounded in your body, so you can connect with your higher self, the soulful version of you that is always present." He adds, "Over time, you will begin connecting more easily with the spiritual realm."

We talk about the powerful energetic field that extends six to eight feet from the human body. From time to time I have sensed that energy around me. Through meditation, I will focus on using this energy field to keep me centered and focused in the moment.

Wes introduces the first meditation in a series of several volumes that make up the meditation program. Sitting across from me, he will participate in the same meditation. Through this shared experience, he will energetically support me in going deeper into the experience.

I close my eyes and settle into the gentle voice of a man beginning a meditation about being totally present in the moment. The voice guides me to focus my awareness on my internal energy and the energy that surrounds me. A few minutes into the meditation, I am finally relaxed enough to sink deeply into the experience. I begin to visualize myself as a strong sturdy tree in a forest. My roots are planted firmly on solid ground and no one can push me over. My leaves may sway but I am always rooted; others can rely on me for that solid presence. It is comforting, affirming, and very relaxing.

Throughout the meditation, I try to stay focused, and yet my mind has its own plans and engages in mindless chatter: *Why am I doing this again? What am I supposed to get out of this?* Though I am grateful for the experience, I am also frustrated. When will that distracting internal voice go away?

A Spiritual Upbringing

My mind wanders to my childhood, where I was raised in a Lutheran church-going family. I remember my father giving layman sermons from time to time during my early teenage years, at the invitation of his best friend who was the minister at our church. Through my father's sermons, he offered deep and philosophic insights that I was unable to understand, but I marveled at his ability to speak so effortlessly. He was creative and smart, with a larger-than-life personality. In his youth, my father considered becoming a minister, but ultimately pursued a more practical path of joining the navy and working for years in the business world before creating a photography business with my mother. He was a choir director, as was my mother, and they made sure all of us sang and were in church each Sunday.

Then, when I was nineteen, my father died unexpectedly at the age of fifty, following several months of illness. My mother, a young widow at forty-four years old, was left to pick up the pieces with three of us five siblings still living at home. It was a dark and scary time, yet I watched in amazement as my loving and highly organized mother rose to the occasion, continuing to build the business and keep our family together while she grieved the loss of my father.

The Lutheran church teaches that if we have faith in God, we will go to heaven when we die and will live there forever. As I child, I believed that heaven was a place far away where we would reunite with loved ones who had passed before us. And that was that.

But I always wondered, what *really* happens when we die? Are we gone forever? Is that it? Can we come back to earth? Do we reincarnate? Can we communicate from heaven with our loved ones on earth? I think we can, but then, I am not so sure.

I want answers to these questions without having to leave earth to get them. I am a seeker. My Lutheran upbringing taught me that there is eternal life in heaven, but there are rules governing that place. Hell is for those who misbehave on earth. Angelic status is for those who lead a stellar life of service. And there's a kind of wonderland for everyone else.

I want to know what eternity is like, without having to experience it firsthand. I want to know that I have direct access to my relatives and friends who are departed. Over the past few years, I have felt the presence of my father around me from time to time and have convinced myself that it was just my active imagination.

A Visitation from My Father

Years ago, I spent the weekend at my friend Jeannie's townhouse in the rugged hills of Turtle Rock in Southern California. We were coworkers at the time and good friends, and I was excited to visit her in the early spring to soak in the warm California sun at Laguna Beach. The California coastline is one of my favorite places on earth and I find the pull of the ocean energizing and also deeply relaxing.

Jeannie and I had a late dinner Friday evening, laughing over old memories and catching up with each other's lives. Later that night I settled onto a comfortable couch in her elegant living room and quickly fell into a deep sleep, the sliding glass door opened to the cool evening air.

Early Saturday morning I awoke to the magnificent view out the sliding glass door overlooking the gorgeous hillside. Bright sunlight streamed through the doorway as I lay quietly on the couch knowing that it would be hours before Jeannie would be awake.

Suddenly I had an unexpected vision of my father slowly floating through the doorway and settling down on the glass coffee table right next to me. I was so startled to see him and tried as hard as I could to bring his lifelike presence into a full human body that I could reach out and touch. He looked so real to me—though he had passed away years before. Why had he come to visit me in California? Did he sense that this would be a place far from my distracting home life where he would have my full attention?

As I lay still on the couch, I heard him speak to me through a voice inside my head. He calmly asked me if I wanted to know why I had been born to him and my mother. *Good!* I thought. *I'll finally know what I'm on this earth to do.* I waited in anticipation for a message that my life might take a new direction because there was something substantial I was to do or create for the world.

Then I heard him in a clear voice telling me *The reason you were born was to bring joy to the world … be joy, live joy, share joy. That is all.* He paused for a moment to allow the message to sink in. I waited in anticipation for more details—a list of things I was to do. But he remained silent and a few long minutes later, his image slowly faded away.

I lay deep in thought for a long while, stunned by his visit and his message. Frankly, the message seemed too simplistic and I was somewhat disappointed. Where was my big mission? Important leadership roles? Groundbreaking discoveries to be made? Was it possible that the only reason I existed was *to be and share joy*? I couldn't fathom that my life was meant to be so simple, though I now know that living in joy and spreading it is not as easy as it seems. This world brings its own set of challenges that sometimes makes it difficult to even find joy, much less to sustain it.

From time to time over the next several years, my father would appear to me when I least expected it, and always when I was near the ocean. Somehow, he must have known that I was most receptive to sensing his presence as the ocean waves crashed on the shore.

Me and my dad

Taming an Active Mind

Throughout the week I work diligently on the meditations. Twice a day in the morning after I wake and in the evening before going to sleep, I listen to the meditation recordings on my computer or my cell phone. Then I quickly capture what I have experienced in my journal to debrief with Wes at next week's session. Often, my distracted mind wanders to more earthly tasks: *Have I turned off the coffee maker? Do I need to stop for gas in the morning?*

Other times I stay focused throughout the meditation and it is then that I feel the very top of my head tingling while I listen to the recording. I'm not sure why. Is this brainwashing? Or maybe *soul* washing? I feel supported, curious, and open. Very relaxed. Yet, I wonder about this connection. The tingling has caught my attention and brings me into a more expanded awareness of everything inside and around me.

One evening during a gentle meditation, with beautiful music playing in the background, I find myself floating on a big yellow cushion on a crystal blue lake. Warm sunshine beams down on me and I feel rested and relaxed while the cushion buoys in the water. As I surrender to the moment, I feel grateful at the thought that I might be able to radiate energy outward from myself. Maybe if I learn to shift my energy to a higher level it will spread to others to help them increase their awareness and learn to be more present in the moment—a good trait for all of us to embrace.

I am getting somewhat comfortable with the idea of not knowing what is happening, what is going to happen, what I am learning—hmm! Is this a bit of my controlling self, releasing its grip? The meditations are grounding and I feel more solid and focused in my physical form—but so far nothing profound is happening. I work on stilling my chattering mind as I am guided through the meditation recordings, yet I question what results I am after.

As the weeks go by, I diligently practice the meditations in a darkened room, eyes closed, with a newfound commitment to not letting myself get distracted. (I quickly learn that my cat cannot be in the same room when I am meditating as he, too, is immensely curious and insists on jumping into my lap, purring loudly.)

Immediately upon completing the meditations, I journal about what I have experienced. The thoughts come quickly and surprise me with the insights I gain that help me understand my behaviors and the motivations that influence my life.

An Introduction to Coach

In journaling over the years, I maintain an ongoing dialog with a voice in my head that seems to come from a different place than where my imagination resides. Is this a guide from the spirit world? I call this voice Coach, and he supports me as I write, posing questions along the way, and contributing wise insights.

One day, years ago, I was surprised to hear a clear voice in my head speak to me while I was journaling. I had been writing about my frustration over what to do with my business as a self-employed career coach, as self-employment left me without coworkers and opportunities to collaborate. I felt disheartened and stuck, wondering what changes I could make.

As I journaled, I thought about how great it would be to be working through this issue with a personal coach. I wrote in my journal, "What if I were coaching myself right now? I would let myself dump all of the angst about feeling rudderless without an employer to call home." And then I imagined a coach saying, "What is it like to feel rudderless?" And I would answer, "scary, frustrating, unfair, hard, makes me sad, makes me feel time is running out and all of this consulting work has amounted to nothing." Then for good measure, I might add, "I feel like a career failure."

I paused for just a moment, back then, and suddenly I heard a clear, calm voice in my head with a comment and a question for me. I was startled and was sure that I was imagining the voice, but I decided to call that voice Coach and I recorded our dialog.

COACH: Interesting … wallow there as long as you need to, to get it out of your system. What do you desire, moving forward?

ME: A balanced life. Time to travel, learn, be with people. Work that makes me feel really good about my contributions and pays me handsomely for the efforts I put into understanding human nature and using those insights to guide others.

COACH: That's good. You've touched that passion for psychology again. I know that it is the thing you love to do

24-7—to help people by sharing glimpses of insights from their behavior so that you can support them. So, what stops you from absolutely embracing this work and continuing to share it with the world?

ME: My own insecurities. Am I insightful enough? Does what I offer add real value to another? What value is placed on wisdom?

COACH: Well, I don't know those answers but how could you find out?

ME: Hmm … (Now I quickly jot down five ideas.) Well, there! I feel a little better.

COACH: Wait a minute—not so fast. What is your plan? What will you do next?

ME: Well, there's a bunch of things I can do. (And I jot down several more ideas.)

COACH: Sounds good—you'll be busy. Be patient. You are in deep learning and processing right now. You need to think about what you desire from your work. What kinds of collaborations? What do you want to build? Where do you want to do your work? Who do you want to hang out with, who are the people who will keep inspiring you to learn?

ME: Okay—so back to today, here is what I will do to take care of myself so that the answers come to me.

And I proceed to end our journaling session with several self-care ideas.

Now, years later, Coach is always my go-to companion in journaling. I like to open my journal, close my eyes, and then write down a question or issue that has been weighing on my mind. Coach instantly responds with a question, observation, or challenge to bring me further and deeper into the topic at hand. I record our back-and-forth communication until we are done conversing. He brings me to a depth that I would likely not achieve on my own.

Other times, I merely begin journaling with no agenda and the voice of Coach is there to ask me the first thought-provoking question.

Practicing Non-Judgment

I am beginning to look forward to my twice-daily meditations. They are a good distraction from my life and allow me a brief respite from the grief I feel.

A week later I am settled into the big leather coach debriefing with Wes on how my week of meditation has gone. "I'm working hard at this. It's new to me, but I think the meditations are making me a little more focused and relaxed than I am used to," I say.

Wes tells me that over time we will be working on non-judgment. To go deeper spiritually, I am to observe and experience—not judge situations or others. "How is that possible?" I ask Wes. "My astrological sign is Libra ... balanced scales ... sign of justice and fairness!" I naturally scan the environment looking for people or animals being mistreated, bullied, hurt. I am pulled by important causes ... social justice, righting society's wrongs. And then I want to step right in—holler if I must—until the unjust has been righted.

Wes replies, "If you stay in either-or thinking, you will not be able to access the creative part of your life. You need to learn to drop all judgment—be open to whatever comes."

I push back. "How can I stand back and do nothing when something is so obviously wrong?"

Wes sighs and gives me a look that says *Oh, you have so much to learn.* "You are not doing *nothing*," he says. "Your role is to send energy and love—not allow yourself to be dragged into the drama. You do not know the whole story. You do not know what lessons those involved in the drama are learning."

I remain skeptical. To wrap my mind around this concept is going to require some deep thinking.

We will work again and again on the topic of non-judgment for the many months it takes me for my perception of judgment and non-judgment to shift.

An Introduction to Subpersonalities

The following week Wes and I experience a guided imagery meditation on subpersonalities—those aspects of ourselves that live unexamined in our unconscious minds. By accessing subpersonalities that reflect our beliefs, typically unavailable to us on a conscious level, we can better understand the drivers of how we behave and interact with others. I am willing to dive in and cannot wait to see who or what shows up.

After closing my eyes and relaxing into the meditation, I am led into a scene that brings me face to face with one of my subpersonalities. I am guided to imagine myself standing in a beautiful meadow, simply observing what appears around me. I look over the field of green grass to the horizon. Suddenly I see a vision of myself in a buttoned-up business suit walking with a deliberate and quick stride across the field. I look so out of place in the serene environment. I know instantly that it is *Judgmental Me*, who is serious and critical and wants to right what she personally thinks is wrong.

Given my new learnings about practicing non-judgment, I want to reject this subpersonality and have her leave (she is embarrassing me), but in the meditation, I am encouraged to embrace her. I reluctantly do so and realize that Judgmental Me is only worried about losing control of the situation and needs to be healed of this.

The meditation continues. Judgmental Me disappears, and the next subpersonality appears on the path. I immediately see that it

Meeting subpersonalities

is Scarcity. *What? Where did Scarcity come from? I thought I had dealt with Scarcity in my life!* But here is Scarcity and I must embrace her before I can move on.

These characters are disarming, and I want to take a class or read some books and get to the bottom of why these subpersonalities showed up.

Wes says, "Do not take on more learning from the outside in. Rather, focus now on your inner healing and raising your energetic vibrational level." He tells me, "We are going to work on seven vibrational energy centers and three light body centers throughout your body over the next several months until you integrate them."

I am grateful to write this down to review later as I have no idea what he is talking about.

Throughout the week I do more meditation sessions with sub-personalities, and I meet a clever, manipulative fox, an annoying skunk, and then an armadillo with a cumbersome shell on its back that must be peeled away. The message I energetically receive from the armadillo is *Let go of your ego trying to protect you and connect instead to the higher realms.*

The final visiting subpersonality that shows up in meditation one day is a large turtle slowly lumbering down the path. Suddenly a huge angel appears on the path right behind the turtle. She is beautiful, statuesque, light, and airy, with translucent wings, and a milky presence. She has come to help the turtle move along the path.

Toward the end of this meditation, I am guided to a mountaintop to meet a master spiritual teacher. I place the turtle in a small pack close to my heart and bring it up the mountain with me. At the mountain top, another angel emerges from the turtle's shell. She is stunning—her skirt shimmers with iridescence; she has a wand and a gentle, commanding way.

She wants me to emerge and be light and sparkly and gorgeous. She transmits a question to me: *What will lighten you to emerge from your shell?*

In that moment I know that movement will help me emerge—gentle swirling and dancing, a beautiful dress, light and healthy food, lots of water. I need to lighten my body to support my "light body" and my vibration.

Wes tells me, "Your spirit needs to feel safe in your body. You must align your emotional centers of love and fear, bringing them in synch with one another." He then tells me, "In the Native American tradition the turtle is the Messenger and he carries great wisdom. In the ancient traditions, a turtle rock carries the wisdom of the ages." A turtle rock is a unique rock structure that resembles a turtle shell. It is believed to be formed by nature through a weathering process involving water percolating through cracks and individual grains in the rock, separating layers of the rock and producing a rounded shape.

I marvel as I think about the vision of my father when I stayed with my friend in Turtle Rock. The connection is not lost on me.

I so appreciate these insights and am grateful when Wes shows me the turtle rock that he has anchored in his garden. His turtle rock was given to him years ago and he tells me that tradition says that you cannot seek to find your own turtle rock. It must be gifted to you.

Age-Regression Meditation

The following week, Wes and I are working on a guided meditation called Age Regression, in which I am guided back in my life to a time when I have felt strong emotions. Immediately, I am reliving the intense emotions surrounding my divorce years ago.

In the meditation, I am in a dark cold dungeon back in medieval times. In front of me is a prison cell with a heavy oak door and a small barred window located too high up for me to see through. The door is bolted shut and my former spouse is inside. I am yelling and pounding on the door for him to listen to what I am saying. Though I know he can hear me, he does not respond. Then again, how am I so sure he understands what I am saying?

In an instant, we switch roles. I am now the one locked behind the prison door. This feels familiar. Somehow, I know I have spoken up in the past about my deep intuitive insights and have been imprisoned for it. Though someone is shouting at me from outside the door, I cannot understand the words they are saying, so I do not respond.

Suddenly I have a moment of clarity about my strong expectations in this earthly life. Though I can so easily form a judgment about who is right and who is wrong, there is so much more that I cannot see or hear that impacts my reactions.

Assumptions about who is right, who is wrong, who is listening, who is not, lead me to believe that I understand what is going on in any interaction. Unfortunately, this leads to a limited view of relationships and the world around me.

Sometimes I am the prisoner, sometimes I am the guard. Sometimes, though I listen, I do not hear.

I'm Starting to Get the Hang of This

By late February, a month into my meditation practice, I am getting used to quieting my mind and calming myself enough to quickly sink into a meditative state. I feel the slightest fluttering of energy inside me, but at the same time, my ego-mind remains restless. I must concentrate hard not to get bored. But if I concentrate, I am thinking. So instead I must let go—loosen up muscles in my shoulders, neck, back. Breathe.

I am working on the Age Regression once again and this time, anger flares up in me. I am thinking about the heated politics, terrorists, those who shout, bark orders, ridicule, bully, and "puff up." This rage and feelings of being out of control and unable to change others is a familiar feeling.

During my childhood, many fathers went off to work while mothers stayed at home raising the children. Any misbehavior by the children during the day was addressed when Dad came home from work. In my family, there were many rules, and compromise was not an embraced concept. I recall my father's booming voice over the dinner table as he reprimanded my older brothers and sometimes me. A strongly empathetic child, I easily absorbed the thick tension that surrounded us and saw that there was no opportunity to explain what had happened or bring the dinner conversation back to equilibrium.

As an adult, I understand that my father just wanted the best for his family. He wanted to keep us safe. Yet I dreaded the dinner hour, anticipating what might occur.

I always wondered, *Isn't there a better way to communicate, collaborate, hear things out?* I learned to fear voices raised in anger and realized that it was best to remain silent. Now that I am an adult, I wonder, *Why have I allowed this fear to stay with me?*

Looking back, I believe my father's anger was about something deep within his own personal memories. Past lives? The need to have things "in control"? Maybe if I had five kids, I would lose it too, wanting to keep everyone safe and under control. Maybe my father was just overwhelmed with the responsibilities of supporting and raising a big family.

Later in life, I learned he had occasional bouts of depression and mood swings in his youth. I can imagine that those feeling created a deep desire to control life. Have I inherited this from my father? Though he has been gone for many years, I know he is constantly with me in spirit and knows I have struggled with my inability to communicate with him when he was on earth.

Beyond the Veil

Chapter 5

Lucid Dreams—Spring

Opportunities and Decisions

It's the beginning of March and Minnesota's snowy winter is melting a little more each week. I am getting more settled into meditation and I am immensely grateful for Wes's soulful guidance. I relish this permission to venture deeper into a mystical world that I have always loved … to discover the things not available through either human sight or our conscious mind.

I keep a watchful eye out for workshops and events that call to me and I notice that there will be an opportunity in June to attend spiritual development training with Suzanne Giesemann, a highly acclaimed spiritual teacher, psychic, and medium. It is to be held at Unity Village in Kansas City, Missouri. A friend and I eagerly sign up for the session and plan our eight-hour drive to the weekend training program.

I have also decided that this fall I will finally walk a portion of the 500-mile Camino de Santiago Trail, taking the "French Way" through Northern Spain. I have been thinking about this trek off and on for a few years now, since talking with a friend who completed the trail and was wildly enthusiastic about it.

This will be the one-year anniversary of the tour I took to Spain with Irene. I feel called to take this journey along the mountainous terrain to challenge myself, reflect, and perhaps spend more time connecting with her.

My friend Lory will walk the entire 500 miles of the trail and I will meet her 125 miles before our final destination at the Cathedral de Santiago, where it is believed that the remains of St. Thomas the Apostle were buried centuries ago. Walking the Camino Trail is considered by many to be a religious pilgrimage. It will be physically and emotionally demanding, and I am up for the journey.

A pile of spiritual and transformative books is growing at my bedside and each night I read bits of wisdom from old friends: Michael Newton's *Journey of Souls* and *Destiny of Souls*; David Weiss, MD's *Many Lives, Many Masters*; numerous books by Dr. Wayne Dyer and by Don Miguel Luis.

Gradually a second pile of books is emerging from spiritual teachers and prolific authors: Suzanne Giesemann's *Wolf's Message* and *Messages of Hope*; Echo Bodine's *Echoes of the Soul* and *What Happens When We Die*; Paul Selig's *I Am the Word* and *The Book of Love and Creation*; and now Shirley MacLaine's *The Camino*.

It seems there is no end to the thought-provoking questions about consciousness, the spirit world, healing energy, and communicating across the veil. I am a willing student and I can't get enough.

The First Lucid Dream

It's been three months since Irene passed and not a day goes by that I am not thinking about her and wishing she were still here. So often I feel her presence around me, but I have yet to hear her voice communicating with me.

One night in mid-March, sound asleep under heaps of blankets, I am suddenly jarred awake from a dream so intense that I know I will never forget it. My heart is *racing*! Irene has come to visit me in my dream, the first one I have had about her since she passed three months earlier. Everything appears so real that I feel as though I am alive in the dream and so is she. I commit to memory everything I can about the surroundings, our conversation, and what transpires so I can record it later in my journal.

In the dream, I am sitting at a small round table eating lunch in a noisy hospital cafeteria when I look up and see Irene enter and walk straight toward my table. I am shocked! I cannot believe she is here! She looks healthy and vibrant and is looking me right in the eyes as she walks toward me smiling. I leap up to wrap her in a huge embrace and in the dream her body is warm to my touch when I hug her.

This is the Irene I have always known, full of energy and life! She excitedly asks me to go get Sarah and bring her to the cafeteria. I tell her that Sarah is at work and will be arriving with her friend Shannon later.

We stand alone in the crowded cafeteria. In the background, chairs slide across tiled floors, lunch trays clang as they ride the metal track to the washer. No one seems to notice us. I am dying to ask Irene a million questions and start by asking her if she rides around in my car with me. In her cheery, nonchalant voice she says *Of course!* And I know this to be true. For months I have felt her sitting next to me in the passenger seat of my car, just outside my peripheral vision. I greet her in my mind, *Hi Irene! I'm so glad you're here,* and we take a ride together.

The dream moves ahead and now she is walking toward me from the serving area carrying a tray of food. Suddenly I see part of her body glide through the arm of a person deep in conversation with someone else. He does not notice her passing through. She looks just like herself in human form, but she is also a filmy, transparent illusion—like ghosts from the Disneyland Haunted Mansion. I know that I have created her in my mind, and yet she is also so real wearing her pretty blue blouse and a sparkling aquamarine necklace.

I ask her if she knows she's dead and she replies, *Yes. I know I died* as if it is no big deal. I tell her, *Please keep sending signs that you are still with us!*

She wants me to tell Sarah that she is always with her too. And, it is also very important that I drive her to the airport later: *I have to be at the airport by 8:00 tonight to catch my flight. We can't be late!*

Soon Sarah and Shannon join us at the table. They want to play a game with Irene and she quickly agrees. The game has small wooden disks bearing capitalized alphabet letters stenciled in black. They look like the keys on an old-fashioned typewriter and the girls ask Irene, *Guess what letter we're holding?* with smug smiles on their faces. When they show her, it is a disk with a letter "T" on it (an important image that will show up a week after the dream).

In the next scene, I am on a quest to decorate Irene's new work area on the second floor. I stop first in a storage room on the main floor to look at watercolor artwork. Irene loves bright, splashy colored prints, and I select three coordinated paintings of bright flowers for her office.

There is a lovely, wide staircase leading up to the second floor. The oriental carpet is plush and the solid oak woodwork and banisters feel rich and luxurious. I ascend slowly, paintings in hand, and as I turn to the left at the top of the staircase, I walk into an expansive office area filled with row after row of cubicle spaces for the office workers. No one is here.

I eventually locate Irene's work area against the far back wall of the office. I hang the pictures I have selected for her wall. I also hang a framed poem by Rainer Maria Rilke that hung in her office in her earthly life. Now the poem seems so fitting.

I beg you … to have patience with everything
unresolved in your heart and try to love the
questions themselves as if they were locked rooms
or books written in a very foreign language.

*Don't search for the answers, which could not
be given to you now, because you would not be able
to live them, and the point is, to live everything.
Live the questions now.*

*Perhaps then, someday far in the future, you
will gradually, without even noticing it, live
your way into the answer."*

After her office is arranged, I return to the cafeteria downstairs. I instinctively know that it is an important day for Irene. I notice that she is now dressed in a stylish woolen suit with a pink rose pinned on the lapel. An older man is giving her a warm hug. She starts to tell me about her father and that it is a one-year anniversary for her. There is no further explanation for this event.

Suddenly she looks directly at me and earnestly says, *I'll do stuff for you. Just ask me.* I am instantly reminded of her generous spirit and know that she has figured out the heavenly rules so that she can be a resource for anyone in need.

That scene fades, and now I see that Sarah is standing alone on a big stage wearing a sleeveless dress that she has purchased especially for this special event. The lights in the auditorium are turned down; spotlights flood the stage. Irene walks slowly from the back of the auditorium onto the stage and wraps Sarah in a soft velvet cape.

Finally, I am getting in the car to take Irene to the airport as I awake from the dream.

I lie in bed wide-eyed and stunned about the amazing dream I have just experienced. Though it is the middle of the night, I know it is important that I get out of bed, grab my journal, and record everything I can remember about this dream. I am filled with such peace and hope and am so grateful for her visit. I long to have her visit again and prolong her final departure.

Maybe this is why I've felt so restless these past few days, unfocused and on edge. Maybe there are more incredible dreams to come.

Dream Debrief with Wes

The following Monday I am at my weekly meditation session with Wes. I read my journal notes about the dream with Irene and he listens intently, occasionally asking probing questions and sharing insights.

Some of the dream seems easy to interpret in the light of day. It makes sense that her new office is upstairs and that she is not yet settled in. It also seems logical she would tell me, *I need to leave at 8:00* and would need a ride to the airport as she no longer lives in our physical realm.

Wes tells me, "The pink flower (often a pink carnation) is a symbol of a celebration or a graduation. I believe Irene's soul knew ten months ago that it would soon be time to leave—it is in the contract she signed when she came to earth."

I instantly recall that ten months ago brings us back to early last summer when she first started mentioning that her leg hurt sometimes and that she was getting occasional headaches. Could she have somehow known deep inside that she was beginning a new journey?

Wes tells me, "The warm cape for Sarah is a cloak of protection that Irene is wrapping around her. Irene is working on waking Sarah up so that she can experience her mother's presence, now that her mother is no longer on earth."

Wes asks me how the meditations have been going over the past week and I tell him, "I'm still a novice and I am have trouble believing what I am experiencing in the guided meditations."

"Just go with it and make up the energy until you feel it," he advises.

That sounds crazy to me, but I am on a path and will keep moving ahead on my journey. Wes says I am making good progress—I am an old soul working on re-awakening.

The lights blink below the cupboards.

I can tell that some of this energy work through meditation is starting to impact my daily life. I relax more easily and know that meditation helps me in stressful times to be more aware of what is going on in and around me. I am "allowing" more—getting out of my worrisome thoughts and into the moment. It's a much more peaceful place.

Is the dreamlike visitation from Irene a sign of more to come? This dream felt so real and I remember all of it in such detail. I yearn for more time with my friend.

A Meeting at Tavern on France

A few days after the lucid dream debriefing with Wes, I reach out to Sarah and arrange to meet her and Shannon for happy hour at Tavern on France. "Tavern," as people like to call it, is a fun, upbeat restaurant and bar with great happy-hour food and drinks. It is always a crowded place. Irene and I have met there with coworkers, friends, and family, including Sarah and her friends, many times over the years. It's a great place to gather.

I'm looking forward to seeing Sarah and am also hesitant about how and if I should talk about the dream. I strongly hope that sharing the dream and the many times that I have felt her mom's presence will be uplifting to Sarah and give her some comfort. On the other hand, she is deep in grief and I do not want to upset her in any way.

We sit at a small table in the corner of the restaurant, enjoying happy hour and catching up. A napkin container, condiments, and an advertising card with the restaurant name and daily specials are placed in the center of the square table. It's crowded tonight, and the background noise creates an intimacy for the conversation we are having.

Wine glass in hand, I say, "Sarah, I'd like to share with you the most amazing dream I had about your mom a few days ago. I brought my journal. Can I read my notes to you?"

Sarah quickly agrees, and Shannon is excited to hear about the dream too.

I open my journal and begin reading about the hospital cafeteria and my first amazing contact with Irene in which she walked toward me, and I hugged her warm body. The girls are listening intently. Then I tell them about the game they were playing with Irene in the dream, where they were coaxing her to guess which letter they were holding on the small wooden disk.

As I continue reading my notes, I casually glance down at the advertising card in the center of the table with the restaurant name and logo, and I gasp out loud. Tavern's logo is a capital T in a circle that looks just like an old-fashioned typewriter key—the exact symbol I saw in my dream. I quickly show the girls where I have drawn the image in my journal, and they are as astounded as I am.

How can this be? I dreamed it and here is the image right in front of us! I feel like Irene is sitting in the fourth chair at this table. Was this Irene's way to let us know she wanted to have fun with us at this restaurant the way we had so many times in the past? Why do I feel like she is here?

I finish reading my notes and we talk about what the dream might mean. As we finish our wine, I silently thank Irene and all the guides and angels surrounding us that Sarah is open to hearing these stories. It warms my heart, and I wonder if there is more to come.

Ixtapa, Mexico—A Trip of Memories

It's the end of March and today I am on my way to Ixtapa, Mexico, with Anne and our business associate and friend, Kathy. One particularly dismal winter afternoon a few months ago, we spontaneously booked a warm-weather destination for our yearly business planning session. What would normally take weeks of pondering over locations and dates was decided in less than one hour with dates and airline hotel packages booked.

Now I am introducing them to my favorite tropical vacation place a million miles away from the cold slushy spring back home. For five glorious days, we'll soak up the sun and make our business plans for the year ahead. We'll also walk the beaches, catch sunrises and sunsets, sip strawberry daiquiris poolside, join in water aerobics, have a few beach massages, laugh a lot, and count our blessings.

On the Pacific side of Mexico on the northern outskirts of Zihuatanejo is the small ocean-side village of Ixtapa. Years ago, I heard that Ixtapa was a great escape from the more popular Mexican destinations of Puerto Vallarta, Mazatlán, and Cancun. Sure enough, it is the perfect setting for several days' stay. Quaint open-air restaurants and bars line the cobbled brick streets all within walking distance of the hotel. There is an open market with all kinds of handcrafted gifts and silver shops galore with mountains of jewelry. All enticing.

Four hours after our early morning departure, we are greeted with a blast of hot and humid air as we step off the plane and cross the tarmac to the terminal. We are beyond ecstatic that we are finally here. After a quick twenty-minute cab ride along the outskirts of Zihuatanejo, we crest the big hill that brings us down into the village of Ixtapa.

We are staying at the Krystal, a family-owned boutique hotel right on the beach. I have stayed here no less than seven times over several winters and I feel instantly at home. The warm ocean breeze flowing through the open-air lobby feels divine and beckons us out to the pool.

We are exhausted from the plane ride and after checking in, we unwind in our separate rooms before heading down to the pool and ocean. When I am finally settled into my room and have discarded layers of winter clothing for something more tropical, I fling open the sliding glass door and step out onto a small balcony facing the ocean. Once again, I am in paradise. From this seventh-floor vista, the pool with its sky-blue tiles sparkles and entices. The poolside is dotted with brightly colored lounge chairs and umbrellas, and from my vantage point, everyone looks incredibly relaxed.

Beyond the pool area, steps lead down to the sandy beach and ocean. Small thatched huts offer a respite for enjoying the beach while being shielded from the intense sun. People of all ages are body surfing the rolling waves and lining up to hang glide over the blue waters. Seagulls swoop and dive, letting out their joyous cries as they traverse the beach. The air is salty and humid and so incredibly warm.

As I settle into a chair on the balcony, my mind instantly goes back to staying at the Krystal with Irene just a year ago. We had invited our daughters along on vacation and had a blast for seven glorious days. Each day, we were up at the crack of dawn to grab to-go cups of thick Mexican coffee from the restaurant by the pool and then claim our poolside lounge chairs for the day. Huddled in long-sleeved hoodies, reclined on beach chairs, we would sip our coffee while we watched the sunrise—chatting about how lucky we were to be in this incredible place with our daughters.

Now I feel Irene everywhere around me and it shocks me that she will not be back to this place. I am sad and lonely for her companionship.

I grab my journal and hastily jot down a question to Coach— *Why did Irene die? Why did she leave so soon?*

No sooner have I written the question than a response comes into my head and I hear Coach guiding me.

COACH: Well, we don't have answers about those specifics. Death is just another human experience. The real question is—How has Irene's death impacted who you are?

ME: Well, it reminds me deeply that our number is up when it's up. Also, it tells me to sprinkle gifts of love and care for others throughout my time on earth.

COACH: And what about Sarah? How will you take her under your wing? She is sad right now—and trying to make sense of everything. What does Sarah need or desire from you?

ME: I suppose an ongoing connection to her mom, to relive the good memories, understand the person her mom was, even more. Be a strong tree she can lean against.

COACH: Irene is helping you now from behind the veil. She sees you are a messenger and wants you to use your strong intuition to know when Sarah might need support and how to be that support. Irene has already hooked up with many angels and helpers. They will allow you to see more and more—and you must be a solid, grounded presence to access this work.

ME: Wes says the right people are coming into my life now. All are here on purpose and they seek me out.

COACH: Find a green glass object in Ixtapa—a symbol of your increasing intuition and clarity. Anne will help you to trust the messages AND trust the messengers.

ME: I'll be thinking a lot about Irene in the next few days. We had so much fun with our girls last year. I can't believe Irene isn't here.

COACH: AND—you'll be at the powerful ocean. Listen to the waves break. Hear and see all of the messages we'll be sending. There's a new direction you will be taking soon. "Figure it out" by going inward through meditation, and be on high alert for messages coming in.

Let's have FUN! Record what you see and hear—it will make sense later.

An Early Morning Dream

A few days later I awake just before dawn and head out the sliding glass door to the balcony, journal in hand. It's quiet except for the sound of birds and the ocean far below. Waves roll in and crash against the shore. Seagulls greet the day. The energy feels overpowering and the view is mesmerizing.

Yesterday, Anne and Kathy and I lounged by the pool, swam in the cool water, walked the sandy beaches, and conversed as good friends do on vacation. I told them both about the messages I got while journaling and later, how, while strolling through gift shops, I found the perfect green mosaic heart to remind me of my journey to greater clarity and insight.

Irene came to visit in a vivid dream early this morning and I am beyond excited. I was so hoping she would be along on this trip. In the dream, Anne, Irene, and I are at a professional business gathering in a large hotel conference center. We are wearing business attire and as we stroll through the crowd, Irene is describing to us what life is like on *the Other Side*. She is content—matter of fact—as she relays her thoughts.

She is so glad to see old colleagues and former clients. I walk closely beside her and from time to time point her out to people in the crowd: *Look—it's Irene!* I say. I want everyone to see that it is her, but the people just look blankly in the direction I am pointing. They obviously do not see anything and have no idea what I'm talking about.

I sit in silence and contemplate this beautiful morning and when I finally open my journal, I write a quick note to Irene.

ME: Thank you, Irene. I am so grateful for these dreams. Your presence is so profound and fills me with gratitude and awe. Is there something you want me to do for you? Messages for others? Help and love for Sarah? You are my friend and I don't really think you've gone anywhere. I know you are NOT here—yet you ARE here—just a dream or a vision away. You have so much wisdom to share. I wish I could remember more of your dream messages to pass along to others.

I look up from my writing and I see that the sun is just cresting the horizon over the jagged rocks down on the south side of beach. This will be another perfect day of relaxation with the hot sun and clear skies. I am enriched, grateful, and restored. The meditation work seems to help center me and fill me with energy. I close my journal and am ready for another magnificent day.

Ixtapa at the break of dawn

A Thought-Provoking Workshop—April

Days later we are back home from our Mexican vacation, and I am restless for more deep learning. I want to continue exploring the spirit world and gain more insight into why Irene and I are experiencing this strong connection.

One morning, warm mug of coffee in hand, I am perusing *the Edge*, a local metaphysical magazine, when I am instantly attracted to an article about Dr. Todd Ovokaitys, a renowned researcher and MD from Johns Hopkins University School of Medicine. The article describes his groundbreaking work developing a unique sound technique that positively affects our DNA and activates our pineal gland to help us reach higher levels of consciousness and well-being. According to Dr. Todd, we only use 30 to 40 percent of our DNA, and the musical tones he has discovered activate and awaken us to higher levels of consciousness.

I am instantly fascinated as I know nothing about the pineal gland or his scientific research for that matter. My intuition tells me I need to learn more by attending his upcoming workshop, "Immersion in the DNA field: A Pineal Tones Rehearsal Seminar." I read, "This workshop is a direct transmission of frequencies or DNA sound codes, of which there are 33 now ... gifting you with accelerated spiritual growth.... Biological studies in plants have shown that the beneficial effects of these patterns reach and even exceed the effects of playing Mozart."

I am riveted. I know that music stirs something deep inside me. Could this be another important piece in deepening my spiritual development?

I plead with Anne. "Come to this workshop with me. It's going to be amazing! Let's just see what it is."

She reluctantly agrees. Although I am sure it will be fascinating, Anne says, "I don't know if I can sit still for two days, but I'll try." Anne is a visionary and futurist, ready to move to action at any moment. We'll see how she does.

When we are settled in the hotel conference room early Saturday morning, Dr. Todd walks into the room and onto the stage, and it seems that everyone in the audience already knows and loves him. They are overjoyed to see him, and the atmosphere is upbeat, full of anticipation for what we will be learning. Dr. Todd is energetic, highly engaging, and extremely bright.

Throughout the day, we receive a crash course on the pineal gland, which is roughly the size of a pea and in the shape of a pinecone. It resides in the center and right behind our foreheads and, as I understand, it is believed to be the place from where we access higher consciousness. We learn 33 Pineal Tones™ Dr. Todd has discovered that activate the pineal gland.

He tells us that some time ago, during meditation, he had a vision of how the coils within the coils of DNA transmit and receive messages to all cells in the body. The tones are intentional patterns that tap into the active codes and activate DNA.

Each tone is a sequence of unusual sounds and melodies that sound haphazard and meaningless to me. They are all sound and no words. Prior to practicing singing each tone, we learn the intent of that specific tone. It may be about "clearing the unconscious blocks to human ability" (tones 27 and 28 together) or "building a bridge to enlightenment, transformation, and healing" (tone 9).

I try my best to internalize what I am learning, but the information is so new to me and it all seems meaningless until we start singing the tones. Then I feel transported to a different place inside my body. It is incredibly relaxing and moving, and I eagerly practice the tones with my fellow students throughout the day.

Anne, on the other hand, is having a totally different experience. For her, the tones are fingernails scraping a chalkboard. She is uneasy and antsy, and at the end of the day, she bids me farewell, telling me she will not be returning for the second day.

Sunday brings more practice singing the tones and I am in heaven. We learn much more about Dr. Todd's breakthrough medical work, but I have a difficult time following what I am learning about his scientific discoveries and their applications. I remind myself that it's okay that I am not scientifically minded … perhaps I have other talents.

He tells us about the Crystalline Choir that is composed of members from many countries who sing these tones in performances around the world. I instantly perk up. I love to sing, and I am intrigued with joining a global choir.

In June, the Crystalline Choir will perform in Hot Springs, Arkansas, and I instantly know I will be attending. Hot Springs and the hotel where we will perform are near Mount Ida, a place known as the quartz crystal capital of the world. Perhaps the crystal will amplify our voices far beyond Hot Springs and bring peaceful energy out into the world. We could certainly use it.

It is difficult to put into words why I am so moved by singing the tones. The tones bring me to the same state of awareness that I feel in deep meditation and I want to experience even more. Plus, Irene has been in my mind throughout the workshop and I want to feel her presence even stronger.

An Introduction to the iCloud

On Monday I debrief my weekend of training with Wes, and he encourages me to deepen my learning and exploring. When I tell him about the Crystalline Choir performance, he feels that it will be a powerful experience for me. My mind is made up. I will participate in the Crystalline Choir in Hot Springs in June.

Wes talks to me about "the iCloud"—where guides and masters from across the veil look through the clouds for bright lights (enlightened souls) through whom the guides and masters can present their spiritual messages and guidance to those on earth. Wes says, "Then when we are interacting with others what we say will be heard differently. Like listening to a soulful singer versus someone who sings without soul. Somehow we feel the difference."

Wes says, "We are all volunteers, not victims." The light blinks. "We have come to earth to raise consciousness of ourselves and others."

Today's guided meditation is about Emotional Release and we practice focusing our energy on the various places in our body where we are experiencing discomfort or pain. Wes tells me, "This is how we heal our bodies: by directing our energy and light to the trouble areas (like neck or shoulders) to release stuck energy."

I find it an interesting concept and I commit to trying it several more times this week. Wouldn't it be something if it were just this easy?

That evening I journal with Coach.

ME: Will these meditations also release stuck emotional energy?

COACH: What is it you desire?

ME: Lightness, brightness, to be strong, vulnerable, be everything the moment or situation desires.

COACH: And then what? And why?

ME: To train and teach and lead others. Please download the inspiration to take things to the next level. What is it? Where is it?

COACH: We'll steer you—we'll send signs. Keep doing your work. Just BE. People will come to you and offer their help. There will be opportunities presented. Irene will help. We want you to help us elevate others. It's not long now. You've been preparing yourself. Trust your partners. You will learn and co-create. Drop judgment, assumptions, expectations, control.

Meditation

Chapter 6

A Deeper Dive Inward

Subpersonalities

It's the first of April and I am meditating once again on my subpersonalities. In a guided imagery meditation, I sit calmly in a meadow, watching for an aspect of myself to come walking toward me from off in the distance. Suddenly someone appears and I see that it is *Me*, myself as a small child with both hands holding tightly to strings attached to a bunch of brightly colored balloons. Each balloon contains a spiritual insight. It is dazzling, distracting, and I hear my child-self say, *Look here!* to those who have gathered around. *Will this insight help you? How about this?* as she tugs at the strings to loosen a balloon for each person in the crowd.

Suddenly, I recall a conversation I recently had over lunch with a friend about the spiritual work I am doing. My friend seemed distracted and impatiently commented that the answers I am seeking can be found inside myself if I just pay attention. There is no need to look elsewhere.

I am taken aback as I feel his judgment coming toward me. I realize that my need to zealously share the amazing things I am learning does not resonate with everyone. Sometimes the timing is off. Had I been more aware, I might have noticed that my friend was struggling with his own issues and was preoccupied. Later, I learn that he was having difficulties with a co-worker. When I started sharing my experiences with him, I felt a huge disconnect between us.

At the end of the guided meditation, I move to the top of the mountain once again. My adult self is with the balloon girl—myself as a young girl. A master spiritual teacher clips the strings and the balloons float away. I can contain all of the messages inside myself and share only when the time feels right.

I am back to center once again. I am on my own path of learning and the lessons are sometimes hard and humbling. I remember that we all have a light source inside us, sometimes radiating more brightly from us than at other times. Ultimately when subpersonalities come to the light—even the dark, flat, deformed, slugs, and blobs—there is healing.

Jesus Appears in Meditation

A few evenings later I am deeply relaxed in a guided imagery meditation when suddenly Jesus appears. I am beyond shocked! Isn't he too busy and at too high of a spiritual level to appear to me in meditation? Yet, here he is. I see him as I have always imagined him in my mind—calming, loving, solid, strong. I feel the energy move up my body to my head, and my head is tingling. I am also unnerved and think this cannot possibly be real. Who am I to experience a visitation from Jesus? But then, I know that we all have access to him and his amazing loving force—we just need to ask.

He quickly transmits a message to me. Though I do not hear him speak the words aloud, His message comes with great clarity: *I am here always. I will give you the energy you need until you are able to manifest on your own. When you come from a light-filled, loving place, you walk the earth protected and magnetic. You see where assistance is needed and without jumping to conclusions or jumping in to fix the situation, you radiate warm loving thoughts to de-escalate what is occurring and open the minds and hearts of all involved.*

In this enlightened way, you do my work on the earth plane. You create strong, loving energy, and manifest beauty and calmness. You open your mind to all kinds of creativity and collaboration.

It is time for you to BE. Doing *will take place as it needs to when the time is right. Just focus on Being now—that's all. This is Phase One.*

When I emerge from the meditation, I am deeply humbled. Was that really Jesus? That is impossible! But then, who says that is not possible? I feel as though His message was so simple and profoundly powerful. What have I gotten myself into? How can I live up to these expectations? I am the little girl with the balloons—and then sometimes I am not.

A Cool Place Called the Temple of the Masters

In a guided imagery meditation the following evening, I find myself transported to a grand temple high on the top of a mountain. In the meditation, I am told that we have arrived at the Temple of the Masters.

I am guided to enter the temple through a massive archway. When I reach the top of the stairs, I look around the expansive courtyard with its smooth cobblestones, great vessels of greenery, and light streaming through the pillars and windows surrounding the courtyard. There is a grand marble fountain with clear sparkling water cascading over stone sculptures of cherubs and angels. I am stunned by the beauty and tranquility of this place that I believe has been here for thousands of years.

Next, I am guided to stand in the center of this courtyard and notice that my soul group, the loving souls who have been part of my journey through many lifetimes, is gradually arriving in the center of the courtyard and surrounding me. I see them slowly emerging from the shadows until they come into clear view. There is Anne, of course, and several other close friends and acquaintances in my life. There are also some in the group whom I have never met.

More and more beings begin filling the courtyard until it is overflowing with loving souls. Looking closer, I see that there are silver strings of light that attach me to them as they are attached to the souls behind them just beyond the courtyard. Those behind us also have silver strings that attach their light to those behind them. And the connections go on and on as far as I can see.

I am stunned by the simplicity of this preordained order. I see clearly that when we spread the light—there is a ripple effect to eternity. Layer after layer of us—each one connected to the next.

To the Temple of the Masters

Just as I am pondering where my light comes from, the courtyard instantly clears, and I am again alone with Jesus. Standing in his presence, I am bathed in his brilliant light expanding in all directions. He transmits his powerful energy to me and opens my energy centers (my chakras) so that I can feel the full force of his energy and light. It is a magnificent moment.

Eventually, this scene fades away and I exit the temple knowing that I can return to this amazing place any time I choose and that I am filled with energy and light that can be accessed at any moment.

An Emotional Healing Session

In the second week of April, a message comes to me through a friend that a monk, who is a gifted healer, is in town to provide individual healing sessions. It is said that he provides powerful healing through his hands, moving body energy to unblock stuck energy and to open chakras. Because I am on my 7 Personal Year journey, I decide why not? I have a healing session scheduled for this morning and I am nervous and excited at the same time.

Once I am relaxed, lying on the table fully clothed, the monk begins his work and I instantly know that this will be different from anything I have ever experienced. He is a body-and-soul worker and will work on removing the old energies and toxins in my body that no longer serve me. A gentle and humble man, he moves his hands above my body in sweeping motions as he softly prays aloud for healing. My soul knows that something has shifted in me and I feel lighter and so blessed by this man.

In gratitude, I leave the healing session and drop into a deep sleep for the remainder of the afternoon. The next morning, I feel Coach summoning me and I quickly grab my journal and settle into my big green chair to write.

COACH: What do you think of your healing session? I sent this healer to touch your soul and help you flush out old stored memories that no longer serve you.

It's part of your initiation and apprenticeship. This healer has warm, positive ways, and inner wisdom. He is physically strong and always expresses his thanks for the work he is allowed to do. He knows the most important lesson I can teach you. Your greatest accomplishments *do not come from you!* They come *through* you but are divinely inspired.

ME: What should I do next?

COACH: It is so simple. Don't make it hard. You must stay centered with an open heart and be with the people. Surround yourself with those who want to elevate their energy. They will seek you out. I will send structures to protect you from overwhelm.

All of the compelling visions you have created in your mind can manifest:

- *Total alignment with spirit as your source of unlimited energy.*
- *The ability to discern the power of energy to attract or repel it.*
- *The pure joy of being in real authentic communities of people who love you and whom you love.*
- *The mastery of inspiring huge crowds to share our messages.*

We've been challenging you to go to the people in need in a way that they can hear you. We need help in our professional institutions and in positions of power.

We have put you there to take some leaps … to bring people and your leaders into clear focus about who they are so they can lead in a way that serves the highest good of all.

Yet Another Subpersonality

A few days later, I am once again in a guided meditation back in the beautiful meadow waiting for a subpersonality to appear on the horizon to my right. This time I am drawn to the left and I see that Jesus is coming down the path and He is holding *ME*! I am four years old and filled with joy and bubbling with laughter. As we walk through the meadow, I feel great love and warmth. I am safe, protected, and full of joy. He silently communicates to me that it is time for me to move into my adult body.

Next, Jesus and I move to the top of a huge mountain and in amazement, I look out over a Grand Canyon-like view. It is powerful, an overwhelming view for a small child. I am in awe.

Suddenly I am surrounded by other masters and guides who have come to speak with me. They give me a luxurious burgundy robe with a silk lining and tell me it is time to move beyond childhood wonder and join them in the work they do. They assure me that they will always be with me, will always protect me and surround me so I can do my highest good to help raise the energy and help others whenever needed.

As I am guided to leave the mountain and return to the meadow, I suddenly see that all aspects of my personality form a perfect glass globe that I can hold close to me. The globe is filled with gold dust and liquid and forms a perfect orb.

I feel spiritual support all around me and I wonder, What am I to do now? How can I notice the signs and opportunities?

As the meditation ends, I am filled with gratitude and deeply humbled. Did that communication really happen? Is my egoic mind creating a fantasy for me? I must sit with what I have experienced and see where it leads.

An Exposure to Reincarnation

A week later, Anne has invited me to a by-invitation-only intimate gathering to hear a woman who has come to town to speak about her belief that she is the reincarnation of a famous historical figure who lived years ago. After we settle into couches and overstuffed chairs around the spacious living room, each guest introduces themself. I quickly notice that even in this group of enlightened guests, everyone seems to have difficulty stating what is true for them about the spiritual world and reincarnation. It is hard to describe and is hardly ever the topic of conversation in daily life.

The speaker's story is very compelling. It has layer after layer of evidence that suggests she is indeed a reincarnation of that famous person. We are spellbound as she speaks of her childhood and the past-life memories she continues to experience as an adult, sharing intimate details of people and places that connect her to the earlier lifetime that she believes she lived.

Later at home that evening, I watch a YouTube video where the same woman I just heard speak is sharing her story. Among the many positive comments below the video, someone has written: "It's a bunch of crap." I feel a sudden resistance. I do not want to be fooled or to fool others. Her sincerity rings true to me and the evidence is so undeniable, yet because the spirit world is so elusive, I must take a leap of faith to believe.

I want to speak about what is true for me—without feeling as though I am trying to persuade others to believe the experiences that I am having. I want to be authentic, a faithful believer in God's ways, and speak openly about communicating with souls who have passed. There are those who will not believe, but that is not my concern.

I grab my journal.

COACH: Well, no worries. You are working on all of this now. It will all become easy and crystal clear when these things are true for you:

- *You have no judgment regarding the situations you encounter.*
- *You remember that love trumps fear and good trumps evil.*
- *You know that each person has a purpose for their lifetime and is on their own path to discover that purpose.*
- *You remember that our richest and most productive life is in service of others.*

Don't make this so hard on yourself. Just show up! Who cares if you stumble a little? We all work on self-corrections. No overanalyzing!

A Birthday Brunch for Irene

It's a lovely Sunday morning in late-April and I am at a birthday brunch with family and friends in honor of Irene. It has been four months since she passed, and I have been trying to find the balance between casual chitchat among friends and introducing a deeper conversation about the communications Irene and I have been having.

I want to shout out, *Do you see? There really is eternal life! We really will see those we love who have passed to the other side. It really is just a veil between this world and the next!* But I remain quiet, keeping these thoughts to myself.

Later that evening I grab my journal to write with Coach.

COACH: You seem to be gathering some discernment to use in your work that there is a time to share and a time to remain silent.

ME: Yes, but it's frustrating to me. I am still too much in my head. I need to work on more soulful connections with others.

COACH: Yes! You are starting to get this. You must first connect soul to soul—then you can listen for what is in the heart of another.

Conversation is an exchange. You are not giving a book report or sales pitch unless that is what is being called for—but most likely it is not.

Remember the story about everyone being stuck in the mud, covered with it and unable to move? The enlightened one walks easily through the crowd and no one asks, "How come you have no mud on you?" They just observe, part to let the person through, and then follow behind.

ME: Yes! That's right! I can let go of a long dialog, and just share (or not) that I am developing my intuition and working on my spiritual development. That is it!

COACH: Bravo! Watch your negative thoughts and replace them with new beliefs:

- *We are one and each of us plays an important part in the whole of humanity.*
- *Our internal spiritual wellness is the most important thing during our earthly life.*
- *We serve best through authentic connection—soul to soul.*
- *Feelings are to be felt and shared when needed.*
- *We each have a team of helpers who guide us.*

Wes tells me, "Listen to the voice of your inner spirit—heart energy goes out in all directions and attracts humans; it also attracts mountains, water, anything and everything that vibrates."

The Deer in the Woods

A few nights later I am deep in meditation in search of yet another subpersonality. This time I am guided to an expansive grassy field surrounded by woods. I am standing on a stage that overlooks a sea of thousands of people who are listening intently as I speak to them. I sense that I am delivering messages of inspiration and hope.

Soon I notice a deer coming out of the woods walking slowly toward me. He is a silent, beautiful soul and his presence brings a stillness over the crowd. The deer's slow, quiet movement attracts the attention of the crowd through his strong energy and presence. He could be easily frightened and dart back into the woods—but he gracefully continues walking toward me.

Suddenly I notice that the deer's appearance is changing. Now he has sunglasses on and is wearing a straw hat, and beautiful flowy scarves of many colors are streaming from him. He is attracting me through his stillness and silliness, and is projecting a vibrant, fun, colorful side to the crowds. His presence brings a light, summer-day sense of fun.

The deer is showing me what I yearn for in this life: the ability to bring joy and lightheartedness to others, while also interacting with them from a quiet, authentic place. Is that possible?

The masters whisper to me that they want the deer to amp it up—be even more colorful and fun. Bright colors, engaged, alive, dancing, singing, carefree—and serving others—making a difference.

A few days later, when I debrief this guided imagery with Wes, he says, *The deer is a symbol of a new adventure.* I know I am already on a spiritual journey. What new adventures await me?

Wes and I are working with the concept of staying neutral to the events that occur around us. Wes explains that we first get grounded, focused, and present in our physical body. Then our emotional body surrounds us for the first eighteen inches out from our body; our mental body surrounds us for the next two or three feet and finally, our spiritual body radiates four to six feet around us.

Wes says, "Our spiritual body is trying to teach us something. It formulates frequencies. Our mental body is the guard at the gate—questioning the new energy that enters the space. And

A lovely meadow

finally, our emotional body determines whether the new energy feels like something that is acceptable. Do I believe and accept it?"

In this way, we don't have any attachment to information that is coming to us. We can trust our body to discern.

An Irene Dream—May

In mid-May, I have a brief startling dream about Irene. In the dream, it is a warm and breezy summer day and we are outside lounging on Adirondack chairs in a lush green meadow. We are leisurely chatting with one another. Irene looks relaxed and healthy—like her old self.

In the dream, I calmly say to Irene, *Can I grab your ankle and see if you can feel it?* She lazily nods her head in agreement, and I grab her ankle. When I look up, she is shaking her head: *No.* She hasn't felt a thing, but I have clearly felt the warmth of her ankle.

Once again, I am struck by how strange it is to physically feel someone's warm human body in a dream. I don't recall this ever happening in any other dreams I've had before Irene died.

Irene tells me, "I know when you think about me. Call me by name and I will always respond. I like to hang out with you."

Back to the Temple of the Masters

In another evening meditation session, I am guided once again to the Temple of the Masters. When I arrive, my soul group is there to greet me. We connect our light through the silver strands to those soul groups behind us. Some of the masters and other guides gather us around them. They are asking us to commit to our light body and spiritual path. They tell us we must nourish our bodies—that is all! Ask of everything we ingest, *Is this nutritious for my body? Does it help my light body? Does it give me energy?*

The masters will help eliminate clutter around me so that I stay committed to my spiritual development.

A few evenings later an amazing thing happens during a guided imagery meditation to the Temple of the Masters. Irene suddenly appears as I am settling into the meditation and accompanies me to the Temple, then stays with me throughout the entire guided imagery meditation.

How incredible that she appears as vibrant and engaging as she was in life! She communicates to me that she is teaching and guiding me to spread the accepting, powerful, all-knowing gift of love to all.

She wants me to focus love to Sarah who is trying to understand the meaning of her mother's death. I can simply share with her what I believe about communicating with souls in the afterlife and not have her feel that she must believe it too. Irene says, *I am always with Sarah and know she will grow even closer to me in this dimension. Sarah is so protected and loved. Her father is watching over her too—he sees the beautiful, loving woman she has become.*

Irene lets me know that I don't need to know *how* these messages are happening. That is irrelevant. Only the fear-based ego needs to know. I need to just BE, and show Sarah lightness, warmth, unconditional love.

Taming Judgment

One Monday morning near the end of May, I have a heart-to-heart discussion with Wes about judgment and how challenging it is for me to release it. I tell him how easily I go to judgment and condemnation when it looks as though someone is being mistreated. I consider the facts of the situation and it seems there is nearly always someone to blame. I have been working with the meditation called "Taming Judgment" and I am not sure I can embrace the idea of non-judgment.

I tell Wes, "I am challenged about what to do when I encounter what I believe to be evil." Then I ask, "When is something evil versus when is there merely a learning moment going on? What am I to do? What is my role as a witness? Do I interfere?"

I continue, "Are evil acts (meaning those where one human or group bullies, taunts, belittles another … or even worse, rapes, murders, tortures) to be ignored as part of one's learning? What are the lessons? In a good-versus-evil story, both oppressor and victim are playing a part, but who is the oppressor and who is the victim?"

I quickly share with Wes five challenging episodes that presented themselves the previous day and have caused me to question my role and my ability to be nonjudgmental.

1. A young father told me a story about his three-year-old son who is an empathetic, loving child. An older boy who lives next door asked the child to play in his backyard. Soon other older boys arrive and when the child was on top of the monkey bars, the older boys quickly left to play elsewhere, leaving him stranded and alone. Eventually, the child's mother found him and helped him down, and her response was to take him for ice cream and then to the zoo. The father's response was to buy his son a new toy and not let the neighbor boys play with it. This sign of bullying deserves some retaliation, does it not?

2. A friend explained a legal conflict he was in. He had invested thousands of dollars for a lawyer to write up a legal contract that his employees would sign when they were hired. It stipulated that if he provided his employees with special training, they would remain employed with his company for a year. Recently he sued an employee who left the company and did not honor the contract. The judge ruled against him and the attorney said there was nothing he could do about it. Doesn't my friend deserve compensation for this injustice?

3. At the local government center, two sisters had their children legally removed from their home on the same day. Both of the sisters are addicted to drugs. I feel strong judgments about those women that they have neglected their children. Shouldn't there be a stiffer penalty for their actions?

4. In the past few days, three children in the community have been raped. As I am talking to friends about this, one says that in the past she was stalked by a killer; another friend said she once accepted a ride from a man who pulled a knife on her. I want justice for those who rape and murder. Is this wrong?

5. Two men at a gas station were filling their cars at the pumps. They dumped their trash out on the pavement. A third man came out of the store and, noticing their action, reprimanded them. They beat him until he was unconscious. Where is the justice here?

I know that these incidents have caught my attention on the same day to teach me something, but what is the lesson? What am I to do in these situations? Stand by and witness—but do nothing? Jump in and try to resolve the situation? Be passive? Turn away?

I feel frozen in place. All responses are wrong somehow. How am I to respond? What is the response that de-escalates situations and promotes a sense of oneness?

Wes explains that I do not know any more about the situations I was exposed to. It may look like one is the perpetrator and one is the victim, but how can I be sure of the whole story?

He says, "First, remember the Law of Attraction—don't attract chaos and conflict. Watch what you focus on."

Regarding judgment, Wes tells me, "Do not carry the energy of others. You are here to learn about non-judgment. You are simply to wrap them in light and send prayers their way."

Then he adds, "Focus your energy and continue raising your energy body and vibration, and you can attract help that way. Do not engage in the drama. Imagine a machine or a fan operating at high speed (as in a human drama) and you are standing nearby with a scarf wrapped around your neck. *Do not* get sucked in!"

Maybe I am awakening so that I can experience non-judgment in the face of earthly drama.

The Lights Confirm

The following Monday we work through a guided imagery meditation that helps me encase my body totally with my energy—through my head, along my body, and into the ground. It is feels so powerful.

I'm feeling slightly nauseous and exhausted from all the spiritual energy work. And at the same time, I notice a surge of inner strength that was not there before. I feel calmer and more centered with friends and clients, and I find that I step out of the rush of daily living more easily to experience life from a broader, deeper perspective.

And of course, I want to communicate more with Irene. She's so alive and has great wisdom to share. I know I must be patient. She is not on my time schedule.

Wes tells me, "I was told that you will be teaching what you are learning." The lights flicker spirit's confirmation.

Insights Revealed

Chapter 7

Learning through Experiencing—Summer

A Better Understanding of My Inner Self

Spring merges into summer and I am gaining a better understanding of how my inner self affects and reflects what goes on in my outer world. Our perceptions really do shape our reality. I continue to meditate morning and evening and now I am filling a second journal since Irene's death six months ago.

I settle into my green chair and open my journal to a fresh page.

COACH: So, what's up?

ME: I am working on accessing the grid in meditation. (The grid is described as an energetic field that surrounds us. I picture a large fishnet above me that expands forever in all directions.) I can imagine what the grid might be like, but I have never experienced it firsthand.

COACH: No worries—you are just remembering. Funny trick, huh? We wipe out memories of the times you've lived in the spirit world between your lives on earth. You must rediscover your power and essence in this lifetime and also uplift those around you.

ME: Yes, this is what Wes says. I have lived many lifetimes. I'm not sure why this mystery has taken me so long to unravel.

COACH: Well, humans think about the world in linear time. And now you see how the spirit world is the only true thing and is everything.

A Journey to the Grid—June

One evening in June I am about to take a journey up to the expansive grid work through a guided imagery meditation. After calming myself and settling into the meditation, I am to meet a guide who will take me on the journey. Suddenly, Irene arrives as my guide—a big smile on her face. What is Irene doing here? She tells me, *I will show you around and teach you to send positive energy and love to the earth from the grid.*

What a delight that she's coming along on the journey. As we proceed, to ascend to the grid, we meet with one of the great masters, and I see that it is Archangel Michael. He is taking us deeper into the experience of working with the grid, which I see is beautiful—golden, sparkling, secure, strong, transparent—and it stretches across a vast horizon to eternity.

The grid seems to hold the collective emotions and circumstances people experience on earth. Their thoughts and feelings about these events percolate up and troublesome concerns or worries appear as small bumps on the grid. By focusing my attention in a nurturing and loving way, I can melt them into beautiful gold liquid that quickly dissolves and drops down beneath the grid and disappears.

Archangel Michael gives me a gift and I see it is a magic wand I can use to spread light everywhere or in specific places. But now the wand is transforming into a different object to be held with both hands. At first, it seems like I am holding a small bird. But when I look closer it morphs into the thinnest pair of white gloves filled with an intense light. Perhaps I can infuse light into everything I touch.

The meditation ends and Irene fades away.

Arkansas: The Crystalline Choir

It's mid-June and I am in the quaint southern town of Hot Springs, Arkansas. Rolling hills, blue skies, and a *down-home* feeling. I am here with hundreds of other souls from around the world to learn the full spectrum of pineal tones from Dr. Todd and perform a concert as the Crystalline Choir for the local residents.

We are staying at the historic Arlington Resort Hotel & Spa, the largest hotel in Arkansas, located in Hot Springs National Park. The hotel was built in 1875 and sits on top of the largest quartz crystal cave in the world. Through singing the pineal tones, I believe our performance will have powerful impact on the earth's vibration.

In addition to teaching and practicing the Pineal Tones™, Dr. Todd shares major breakthroughs in rejuvenation medicine that lead to ideas for reversing aging and expanding our awareness and abilities.

We practice for three joy-filled days. Words cannot begin to describe how amazing it feels to participate in this event and sing the tones. While performing one of the tones, I am transported across the diamond grid while the images of my loved ones who have passed greet me at every turn. There is Grandpa, Grandma, my father, my uncle, my sister-in-law, and of course Irene.

Later, as the event winds down, I grab my journal and write with Coach.

COACH: Well, what did you learn from your experience here?

ME: That I was supposed to come—be surrounded by like-minded souls from across the world and sing the tones on this beautiful quartz crystal mountain.

COACH: Tell me about the messages you received.

ME: I can use the crystal bowl (one I purchased at the event) to connect with myself and with others. Maybe I was a minister or spiritual leader in a past life. I know these people—they are familiar. I have been with them before.

The tones are invigorating—the intention strong.

COACH: Okay—so what? Is there something you wish to do with this learning?

ME: I don't know. I'm opening up to being led. I feel my life is changing, shifting, transforming.

COACH: Are you willing?

ME: Try me. And I will remember the wisdom from Wes: *When opportunity comes you must follow it. You are ready or you would not be called.*

Arlington Hotel

The Crystalline Choir

Serving Spirit Retreat at Unity Village

I am back just a few weeks from the Crystalline Choir event in Hot Springs and am on my way to yet another learning event at Unity Village in Kansas City, Missouri, with Suzanne Giesemann, a renowned evidence-based medium and spiritual teacher. She is leading a weekend program called Serving Spirit. Suzanne is committed to verifying the messages she receives from spirit, thereby providing evidence of their authenticity. Our group of fifty-some students will spend the weekend learning about ways to access our guides and departed loved ones.

After an opening session with Suzanne on Friday night, I am back in my room and I open my journal to capture the experience so far.

ME: Well, here I am digging deeper into spirit work again.

COACH: Listen to Suzanne. We have messages for you that will come through Suzanne for all.

ME: Darn, my ego hoped I would get them directly, maybe in my dreams.

COACH: Well, that is curious. What are you so yearning to know?

ME: When will Irene come again with more messages and wisdom? How do I call on additional guides and masters?

COACH: Okay, so you get them on the line and then what?

ME: Well, maybe I'd ask them what I should do with all this knowledge and new experience.

COACH: Well, how about if you decide for yourself? We'll make you a deal. We will do this fifty-fifty with you. You come up with ideas and so will we. We'll present opportunities right in front of you. It will be a game and we will both win because somehow you will continue the work.

Saturday Night Reflection

After a day of intense learning and guidance from Suzanne Giesemann about accessing spirit, I am ready to reflect on what I have learned. Back in my hotel room, I open my journal to write with Coach.

COACH: So how was your day? Tell me about the breakthroughs. You know we need you working at the strongest frequency possible. No worries—we're just guiding you and your companions—spirits guiding you from the other side.

ME: I learned the most important lesson of all today. There is ONLY love! That's it—truly everything else is an illusion. There is NO need to ever feel *less than … I do not* *ever need to experience feelings of abandonment, a sense of being judged, of being not enough, of smallness. I GET IT!*

COACH: So, what shifted?

ME: We can avoid feeling aloneness if we remain aware and attuned to the spirit world. EVERYTHING is alive. All is energy. I am in an energy bubble surrounded by love—and drama, of course, since this is the earth. I choose to be here. I rejoice in the lessons I've learned, and I know there are others opening to learn.

COACH: Progress! Good for you! We made sure you got here in this place and time to hear all that we have shared through Suzanne. She took on the role of channel for our wisdom. What about you?

ME: Well, I know I am to take opportunities as they present themselves. What can I do and how can I be of service?

COACH: Trust that we are right here. We will not let you fall or fail. We are here to help and guide. We think you have learned lots of lessons. Trust what we want you to do. You are a part of us—we could use a spokesperson. There is a lot of elevating and much sharing to do in your world.

ME: Okay, I go to my brain to figure out what's next and I don't think the answer is there. Will you send me more signs and messages about what I need to align with and share?

COACH: In good time—when you calm down and don't act like your life depends on it. There is no specific thing to DO—it's just being yourself—show up—stand in what you know and what you've been shown. Please integrate and in the process, the path will appear.

Remember—when opportunity presents itself you are ready! Give us a summary of what you've concluded from what you've learned.

ME: This is what I have learned.

1. We are both ego and spirit. Depending on which we choose to follow in any given moment, we will shift the outcome of our decisions.

2. There are many levels of helpers in the spirit world: Guides, Angels, Archangels, God. We can ask for guidance at all times.

3. All fear can be transformed through love.

4. By deepening our connection to the spirit world, we can let ego, thoughts, and drama move through us, and we remain strong.

5. Messages and blessings surround us.

COACH: *There has always been and will always be just us together*

Journey to Past Lives—July

This morning, Wes tells me that we are going to experience a guided imagery meditation that will bring us into past lives. I am curious and also skeptical. I do not know how I feel about the idea of past lives, but I am willing to give it a try.

Years ago, I read a groundbreaking book by Brian Weiss, MD, *Many Lives, Many Masters: The True Story of a Prominent Psychiatrist, His Young Patient, and the Past-Life Therapy that Transformed Both Their Lives.* The book chronicles Dr. Weiss's work with a young patient suffering from anxiety and fears. After traditional therapeutic methods failed to produce results, he decided to try hypnotherapy and his patient immediately regressed to another lifetime. Over the following eighteen months, Dr. Weiss documented many of his patient's past lives, accessed through hypnosis. Using past-life therapy, Dr. Weiss was able to cure his patient of her current day issues.

I found the book fascinating, though my mind struggled to accept the idea that past lives are within all of our reach.

Now, I am ready to try it for myself. I settle deeply into the guided imagery meditation and I am eventually led through a doorway into a past life.

A door to past lives

In the first past life—I am walking through a narrow muddy alleyway in the small town of York, England. I am twelve years old and I believe it is the early 1800s. Looking down, I see that I am wearing simple clothing—a burlap covering with rope for a belt. My bare feet feel the damp uneven ground as I walk. I have strongly developed intuition and seem to *know* things about other people without them telling me.

From the whispers of the adults around me, I know that the town is filled with charlatans. It is a chaotic, wild town and there are many who make fraudulent claims that they have psychic abilities and can predict events that will happen to others. Their deception goes unchecked since others are eagerly following their advice.

I speak TRUTH and want to call out the lies I see all around me, but it is not safe to confront and accuse someone of lying or fabricating what is to come. My body carries extra weight—I am protecting my body from potential physical attack when I question what others know. I see people blindly following the suspicious and invented projections of those pretending to be seers, and I want to yell out, *Don't listen! You can decide for yourself!* I have a pure psychic gift and want only to help others.

I move now into another past life.

In the second past life, I live in a village in rural India. I am a young boy of nine or ten. I am slender with shiny black hair, dark skin, and I am wearing a loincloth. Though I am young, I am a teacher in the village. On this hot afternoon, my adult students sit in a circle around me. I crouch down on the dusty ground, encouraging them to use their stick to draw a picture of what exists outside of this small village. I want them to draw an imaginary world where everything is beautiful and thriving.

Every drawing is perfect. It's what they created and now they have a tool so they can go to their imaginary place any time. I am loved and admired for bringing this beautifully simple gift to the people of the village. I am not afraid to be *seen* for my psychic abilities. The people admire me because I help them see beyond what they experience in everyday life.

More Past Lives

A few nights later I am once again meditating on past lives. I relax into the meditation, am guided down a path, and when I open the door, I am in another past life. In this life, I am a young Japanese girl in a beautiful palace high up in the mountains. The greenery and colors around me are vivid and the garden flowers burst with color. I am fifteen years old.

I feel my small feet in pink silk slippers with no arch support. The ground feels hard under my feet. There are several of us who are going to perform a dance to sensual music at a ceremony in the palace for the elders in the village. I see my ornate silk kimono and I can feel the silk sash securing the kimono against my body. We have made-up faces that are painted to be expressionless—but we are full of expression and excited to perform. This is quiet, lovely self-expression within the traditions of the times. We feel honored to perform and are much admired.

In my next past life, I open the door and I am in Paris, France. It is the early 1900s. I touch my face and feel the stubbly beard that I am just starting to grow. I am a tall man with a polished look: cap, knickers, dark woolen coat, a silk ascot. I have on worn black boots that go up to my knees with big silver buckles. I am a poet in my mid-thirties.

Writing poetry is my livelihood and there is pressure for me to be masterful! There are so many others who are famous for expressing through their art. I must keep up to be accepted. I am temperamental, and I flare to anger if my writing is anything less than brutally honest. I abhor trite expression and worn phrases. My poetry is raw and bold and pierces the heart.

As I ponder the circumstances and experiences from my past lives, I see that there are helpful insights about how my behaviors exhibited in past lives impact behaviors in my current life. I see that I carry ease of what I know (teacher in India), a discernment of what is truth and what is not (psychic in York), a joy of life (young dancer in Japan), and a pressure I put on myself to get things right (poet in Paris).

I believe that memories from our past lives lie deep inside us, buried beneath our conscious mind. What amazes me most is that I am always *Me* in my past lives—always myself—and yet my personality, values, and worldview evolve over lives.

A Surprise Visit with Irene

On an early Saturday morning in July, I wake to the tingling sensation once again that lets me know Irene is near. It has been six months since she passed and though I am able to talk with her in dreams and see her in visions, I want a closer connection with her.

I grab my journal, close my eyes, and tentatively begin writing.

ME: Irene, are you *really* here or am I making you up?

(There is a moment's pause when I hear Irene's voice in my head, and I quickly record her message.)

IRENE: *Why would you think that?*

(I am ecstatic! I am actually hearing her voice talking to me as though she is sitting right next to me. Am I just imagining this? She sounds just like she always sounded. No pretense—just her down-to-earth self!)

ME: What can you tell me today?

IRENE: Everyone here is cheering you on and wants you to share what you know about this side. Tell Sarah I am the moths and I am always trying to get near her. Those were moth kisses! (Sarah has talked about a few moths she found in the condo since her mom passed. She cannot figure out where they came from and why they don't leave.)

ME: Why did you leave so quickly?

IRENE: I got the good deal—didn't have to suffer and linger. The people I loved were around me. I saw that Sarah would be supported. I'm busy here doing good deeds for people on earth. I'm gonna get you more help. People on this side know how to do all kinds of things energetically. By the way—Happy Fourth of July!

And just like that, she is gone.

Journaling with Irene Once Again

A few days later, I try to see if Irene will visit me again. I listen to a meditation session to make sure I am deeply relaxed, and I sit quietly until I feel the tingling sensation on top of my head. Then I open my journal, close my eyes and write.

Me: Irene, are you here? I need some confirmation that I'm not making this all up. What's happening? Where are you? I know you are real, but I have doubts about if I just *want* this to be real. Could you bring my guides and let's talk?

COACH: Okay, we're here. What's up? (What? I was writing to Irene. Why is Coach here?)

ME: I am so frustrated, feeling judged by people who want me to *prove* that I really have these connections.

COACH: Ha! Ridiculous! Why does that matter? Could it be you are one who sees? Try to describe the elephant to one who sees only one piece. We are working with you and you must declutter your skeptical mind.

ME: Irene, what do you think?

IRENE: Here is what I can tell you, I saw Debbie (Irene's friend who died several years ago) when I got here, and it was amazing—the best—and she was so healthy! Mom and Dad too—great love and comfort from both of them. They were surprised but were waiting for me and were so thrilled.

There are many great masters here. They are around when we need them. We call on them to help with earthly things.

I like to comfort people, so they feel loved. I get to do that here and I can be all over the place. I've been checking in on my loved ones and wish they would know I am with them.

I'm so glad we had the photo from the cathedral in Barcelona. Like a mirror, I see and feel when my friends and relatives look at the photo and think about me.

It's not that complex. I feel like it's real-life over here. I still get to help others but don't have to get to work on time! Ha! I am just starting to explore. It's kind of weird being so light—but so is everyone else—free and unfettered, soul to soul.

I was at my funeral and know you saw me. Wasn't it great? Loved the eulogies. Sweet Sarah did so well.

I've had a life review and it was pretty good. I got to see my kindness and the impact that had on others. I guess I could have had more confidence, maybe. I don't know where crazy self-doubts come from.

I am so happy you talk to me. We had so much fun on our trips, didn't we? I know you keep me in your mind. I'm grateful you know I'm nearby. We can talk anytime.

I'll try to get some more ideas coming your way. It's all so easy really—just a piece of cake—like being a bird flying around.

I miss you guys but I'm always around you. I will watch out for you—especially on the Camino Trail. In fact—I'll walk with you. My hip doesn't hurt anymore. Ha!

ME: Do you have a team of guides?

IRENE: Of course! You might recognize them. They are all around and very busy. They're the big guns and we bring them near often!

Thank you for being with me at the end. It's weird to float away. You were all there and it was beautiful and so comforting. I love you.

ME: Thank you, dear friend. I know you are nearby. Some time we can go to the movies or out to dinner.

IRENE: Angel kisses!

(I pause as I feel Irene fading away. Then I continue writing in my journal.)

ME: That conversation felt so real. I can't even believe it may not be and that I am making it all up.

COACH: That's just EGO! Remember, you've got an ego just like everyone else, but it can trip you up! You're playing a game on earth. You're solving a mystery, a treasure hunt really, and just when you have great faith, ego says something to you and knocks you off base. Time to toughen up! See through the smoke and mirrors of ego. Be the light!

A Dream at the Log House—July

It's a great idea to escape the summer heat by driving up to northern Minnesota and Wisconsin. I am fortunate to have been invited by good friends to spend a few days at their glorious and spacious log home on the shores of Lake Superior.

We spend our time meeting with friends at a favorite coffee shop, riding bikes through the Superior National Forest, grilling salmon and fresh veggies out on the deck overlooking the woods, laughing, and telling the same silly stories we've told a thousand times before.

On the second night at the log home, I am in a deep sleep when I jolt awake from an intense dream with Irene. In the dream, I am upstairs in the log house where a crowd of fifty or so has gathered. We are meeting as a book club and are discussing important topics about current affairs —though I am not sure what they are. There are guests singing and mingling with one another and sometimes people wander off. We've been on a brief "Black Lives Matter" walk across the bridge that is on the property of the log home. It is a festive atmosphere, and everyone seems to be enjoying the diversity of the crowd and the important topics being discussed.

Instantly the scene changes and now we are all in the lower level of the log home. We are in a college classroom on the exact campus where Irene and I attended graduate school in real life. It is time to say a few closing words to the crowd and I have been selected to do so. All the guests are seated quietly, and I am standing at the head of the classroom delivering my message.

Suddenly a brown-striped silk pillow flies through the open door into the classroom and lands on the floor in front of me. I am astonished and I know everyone else is as well. They quickly stand up to see what has happened as they look in disbelief at the pillow lying on the floor.

I know immediately that it is Irene who has arrived as a silk pillow—just like the one on her living room sofa. She is playing a silly prank. I pick the pillow up and hug her, then start telling everyone the story of her quick death, how she visits me, and the messages she brings.

As I am telling the story, some of the people get up and leave the classroom. They have doubts or don't believe what they just saw. It doesn't align with their belief system. My friends who have experienced a loss of loved ones are visibly moved and in tears about their own losses. They remain in the room.

Irene communicates to me that she wants her presence known if, and when, it can help. She also wants me to tell others about our connection, so they understand. The spirit world is here—we just can't see them—so they work hard to make themselves known and they have so much love for us.

A Breakthrough

A few weeks later, Wes wants to know what I'd like to be doing a year from now. He stumps me with the question, and frankly, it makes me feel a little stressed. I have a challenge projecting myself into the future. I don't really like to think about it—I feel a lot of pressure. He encourages me to give it some thought.

That evening I open my journal and write.

ME: What do I want to be doing a year from now?

(I pause for just a moment pondering the question. No ideas come. Suddenly Coach jumps into the conversation.)

COACH: Why does thinking about your future make you feel nervous and like you don't want to commit?

ME: Because I don't think I am being true to myself all the time. I've been on this journey with you and Irene, and I think I know about communicating with the spirit world but how do I really KNOW? I need as much validation as can be sent, or I just need to trust that this is all the truth and quit pretending I don't believe it!

COACH: There you go. I knew you'd come around. The self-doubt is such nonsense and you know it. You see the lights flashing in Wes's studio whenever you need some support.

ME: What do you want me to do to send more love into this world?

COACH: Gather a group. Start the conversation. Find partnerships and support. Follow your inspiration.

I sigh. It seems easy enough—but I still don't understand how this is all going to happen.

A few days later I am deeply relaxed in meditation and have an amazing experience: my father appears in front of me and he remains with me throughout the meditation. Quickly I grab my journal to record what has happened.

ME: In meditation, I saw my father elevate and brighten until he floated in front of me and I realized that he is a master in the spirit world. Such beautiful white light and strong radiance.

I ask him to help me and guide me so I can remove all fear-based ego from my interactions and only bring love. Dad can help me find my voice and deliver my message.

I am in awe and so excited. This is a breakthrough for me!

COACH: What? What broke through?

ME: Feelings of hesitation, doubt that I can know the things I know.

COACH: But what about your dad? What is the breakthrough there?

ME: We are with each other soul to soul now. He can guide me—he is encouraging me—I just needed to remember who he is—I am so blessed.

COACH: Invite him to be one of your guides. He can plant seeds of inspiration. He sees how hard you're working and wants to do anything he can.

Mid-Summer Malaise

My work week is slow. I could meditate more, but I just want to sit in solitude and reflection right now. I know that this is the most amazing time with such powerful images coming, but I am also living my human existence, working and paying bills.

COACH: I see you putting worry and pressure on yourself— asking *Am I doing enough? Should I be accomplishing more? Why can't I move to action? Blah, blah, blah.*

ME: Well, yes. I am impatient with myself. The clock is ticking. There's much to experience on earth.

COACH: Do you need some guidance from the other side? Do you know how we watch you and have surprises for you when you are ready?

ME: Tell me. Help me be open to a vision or opportunity. What do you and/or they see?

COACH: The masters support you speaking to crowds, gathering stories. Do it your way. How do you want to spread the stories and parables? They are to be shared—they are guidance that people can live by.

What if you created your own parables? We can help plant seeds of inspiration. We want your wisdom and your words to shine the light where there is darkness.

A Morning Lesson

It's a beautiful summer day and I am taking a long walk near my home on a tarred path that leads me beside a small lake, through a city park, and along a wooded area. Early on, I see a homeless man sitting under a bridge eating a sandwich and shouting aloud to no one in particular. I smile at him and he looks up and waves a greeting to me.

I continue walking along the path and soon I pass a young man with long hair, a lanky frame, and a determined look on his face. I glance at him, smile, and say "hello." He says nothing, does not glance my way or acknowledge me, but just keeps walking.

Soon after, I look down to see a painted infinity sign on the path. Instantly I understand the balance in life. In any moment we can engage or hold back, go this way or that. Yet we are all one and no action is any better or worse than the other. It just is.

We cannot make assumptions or judgments. All is as it should be. We can remain neutral, living in the center where we acknowledge both sides.

Forty-five minutes later, I pass under the bridge once again and the man is still talking aloud. I smile and wave. Have a good day!

As spiritual teacher and author Don Miguel Ruiz teaches us: Don't make assumptions! Perhaps the man really is talking to someone.

Soul's Work

That evening, I am listening to a guided imagery meditation that leads me on yet another journey to the Temple of the Masters. When I am in a deeply relaxed state, a guide appears as a beautiful woman from the celestial realms. She leads me to a doorway that I open and I step onto the path of my soul's work in this lifetime. Instantly, I feel a soft, green velvet robe wrapped around me, and I am teaching a small crowd of people—helping them unearth the sacredness within themselves and align with spirit.

I realize in this amazing meditation practice that the answers seem so clear, I need to trust what appears to me and bring these learnings into my day-to-day world.

Exploring Singing Bowls

For a change of pace, I decide to attend a service at a local community spiritual center to experience a new form of meditation through singing bowls. The service is taught by a monk from the local community.

I learn that one way to think about meditation is that it aligns the body's energy centers. Just like a spine—if our disks do not align, our body will be crooked and unbalanced.

When we are in alignment, we increase our frequency and feel joy and gratitude and love. So, no matter what challenges we are facing, we feel peace. Then we radiate this feeling of peace to those around us.

I recall a class I took in college about several forms of meditation, including walking, singing, mindful eating, deep breathing, and many others. It relaxes me to know that I have options.

Later that night I receive direct messages from my guides that I hastily record in my journal.

GUIDES: Hear us fan the flame with sound … Sing! Let the musical frequency interact with the frequency of another. Know we provide the guidance. Get out of your own way. This is not a solo performance. Use the crystal bowl.

Learn more of the ancient customs. Others will connect with the energetic joy you exude. Awaken consciousness through sound vibration. Trust we wouldn't lead you down the narrow path—a road to nowhere. Quite the opposite. There's a choir of sound—heavenly realms. Bring this to earth. Raise the vibration. We'll show you how.

Thank you.

My Learnings So Far

A few days later I am writing in my journal when coach poses these questions to me.

COACH: You've been at this for six months now. What has changed? What are you willing to let go of? What new ways are you exhibiting?

ME: Here are my learnings so far.

- I am experiencing increased awareness and focus on my surroundings.
- I realize that I access connection with the spirit world through the top of my head (crown chakra).
- I find it is easier to release my thoughts in meditation—let them flow through me.
- I see how it is best not to attract, engage in, or create drama.
- It is possible and desirable to send my healing energy out into the world.
- I can self-monitor so I know when I need to regroup and align my energy again.
- It is a good practice to avoid lower energies or help transform them.

- I am becoming more aware of guides, helpers, and synchronicities surrounding me.
- Beautiful music centers me.
- I remember that I choose everything for learning and growth—I need to choose wisely.
- I need to steer clear of judgment and of making others wrong.
- Love is the highest vibration.
- I am evolving to be more open, honest, available, humble.
- When the spirit of competition is "light," it makes us stronger and challenges us to grow.
- Competition at lower frequencies makes the *other* wrong, and we diminish our energy.
- I am on a spiritual journey. There is no turning back or unknowing what I know—only forgetting, and then the meditation brings me back.
- Miracles abound. Perfect teachers are everywhere.

I am working on releasing:

- Defensiveness.
- Letting the need for approval run me.
- Engaging in or creating hype and drama.
- Judgment of self or others, which keeps me small.
- Annoying "brain chatter" during meditation rather than letting thoughts flow through me.
- The idea of "timelines"—that there is a beginning and ending to my spiritual development.
- Comparing my journey to anyone else's.

- Fear-based thoughts and beliefs.
- Dead space—environments of negativity.
- Wondering WHY ME? Rather than why not me?

New ways I am practicing:

- Learning to integrate experiences from many sources (teachers, guides, books, meditation).
- Tuning in to all messages from Irene and Coach and guides, and knowing that these are Divine connections.
- Exercising patience and understanding that the path is unfolding exactly as it should, in perfect timing.
- Being grateful for this spiritual guidance and assistance.
- Trusting my instincts to follow through on the messages I receive.

As I am writing, I sense that the room is filling with souls. Now I close my eyes and see that the souls are parting, and Christ is coming to me and he puts his hand on my forehead and tells me—declares—that it is time for me to see—and then suddenly I am with many others giving me the same message.

COACH: You see through the eyes of your soul to be in service to others. Stand in power and strength.

Speak what you see and notice what *the other* has to say about it.

Keep energy and frequency at the highest levels when interacting with others.

An Early Morning Irene Dream

One morning in early August, I wake from an intense Irene dream. In this dream, I am with several female friends at a large outdoor sports arena packed with people attending a baseball game. Suddenly a man standing near me points toward the top row of bleachers and says, "Look! Isn't that the woman with the red hair?"

I look toward where he is pointing and there is Irene, casually chatting with the people around her. I yell out her name several times, waving frantically. I can't believe she is here! I am dying to go talk to her! She glances my way but does not acknowledge me as she continues talking to the people nearby.

Soon, one of the women I am with says, "Look! There are two of my aunts who passed!"

I look and both aunts are sitting nearby perched on a low cement wall. They are smiling and laughing and waving our way.

Then someone else says, "Look! There is the five-year-old boy who died in our town!"

I look in the direction the person is pointing, and I see a young boy wearing a baseball cap and walking up the cement stairs of the arena holding hands with some family members.

I feel emotional and overwhelmed with this dream. It's one thing to encounter Irene in my dreams, but a whole other experience to witness the departed spirits of others enjoying life among the living.

Do we really all inhabit this earth together … the living and those who have passed? I think we do, but why are we blinded to seeing spirits around us? In my dream, I could see the spirits of those departed as their joyful, human selves. *Can I also see these spirits in my waking hours?* I wonder.

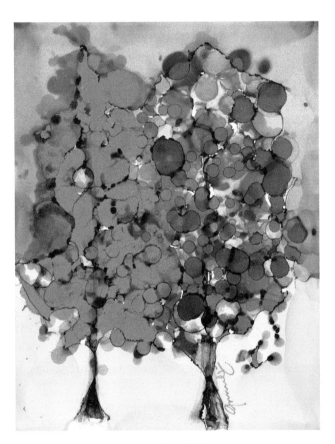

Intuitive Shift

Chapter 8

Acting on Messages Received

Another Amazing Workshop

As I continue my search to deepen my spirituality, another workshop calls to me. It will be held in Madison, Wisconsin, with Paul Selig, famous medium, author, playwright, and educator from New York City. My friend Jana has heard his podcasts, read his books, and is a big fan. I quickly follow her lead and we are on the road for two days of intense channeled messages from Paul's spiritual guides.

After settling into my hotel room on Friday evening, I open my journal and begin writing.

ME: I am here at this retreat—but why? Curiosity? More knowing? Deeper awareness? Favorite hobby? A distraction from real life … or maybe this *is* real life! What is there to learn this weekend?

COACH: Let's start with *What do you want to learn? What is your intention?*

ME: To gain a deeper, more expansive understanding on how to hear, see, and sense at an energetic level.

COACH: Have you figured out why?

ME: I don't want to figure it out. I want to be open and allow and be led by my guides.

COACH: No worries, we brought you here. There is more to know. We are ready to teach. You are ready to learn. Tune in to the energy of the space. Get ego out of the way. Be a channel, let go of *not knowing* and focus on *knowing*. We're calling you out here into expansive space and energy.

The two-day workshop flies by. We spend hours listening to Paul channel messages from the guides. His work with the guides is riveting, and he has transferred their words verbatim into several books he has authored.

Later that evening I journal with Coach and he gives me great guidance.

COACH: You know everything you need to know. Just BE and all will be revealed. The path unfolds as it should. We guide it. You are not saving the world or saving anyone. Merely helping humanity come together at a higher frequency to live in peace and love. You need nothing in exchange. Only ego needs the recognition and awards.

You do not have to be the best at anything—all of that is ego.

Just say "I'm going to the fair ... come if you'd like." Then let it go. It's your Being that will attract others to the path and then they will spread the word farther.

It may seem like you are going alone to the fair and you may be lonely, fearful. Get past that. Your divine self is calling you to the fair for fun, joy, connection. No need to explain or have a PR campaign—just go! Open your eyes to what is in the next place rather than feeling deserted, forgotten, and alone because you have left the group and followed your instincts.

BE BOLD! You are not making mistakes. If you desire to go to the fair, why hold back? To be like others? No, they will have their own fun. Find your community. Others support you as you move toward living life in a whole new way.

A Lesson in Listening

Days later I have my first test to see if I am willing to listen to messages from the spirit world and follow through.

It is a dangerously hot afternoon in August, nearly 100 degrees with high humidity. I am escaping the heat, sitting in my cool air-conditioned house. While writing in my journal, I ask for the ability to hear messages from the other side. Nothing comes to me through Coach or Irene. The journaling feels flat today—I am distracted and unable to connect. I decide enough is enough and close my journal. I will come back to it later.

Ten minutes later I am heading out the door to run some errands when I suddenly hear a clear direct voice in my head. The voice boldly says, *Buy water and hand it out*! I am so surprised at the message and momentarily toss around the idea of dismissing it—then I realize that my first reaction to dismiss an idea may be why I don't hear more messages.

Feeling committed now to the task at hand, I stop at a local convenience store, buy a case of large water bottles and several boxes of granola bars, and start driving around the neighborhood looking for sweaty and exhausted people to serve.

There are no people who are homeless standing at the usual street corners—it's way too hot for them. I pass a construction site and see that there are two shirtless young men directing traffic around the construction. They look like they are sweltering in the heat. I slow down and hand them bottles of water through my open window as they look directly at me with a grateful smile.

I continue driving down the road until I see a man sitting on a curb beside his car in the parking lot of a home and garden center. All the car windows are rolled down—so I assume he has no air conditioning. He is chatting on his phone and I don't want to startle or interrupt him. I pull up beside him, quickly grab water and a granola bar, and offer them with a heartfelt smile. He gratefully accepts the gift, smiles back at me, and waves.

Now I am on a roll, but it is hard to find anyone outside on such a hot day. Eventually, I see a jogger (that's right—a JOGGER!) with no shirt, jogging shorts, and drenched in sweat. I am driving in an area congested with traffic so I cannot pull over, but I am compelled to follow him.

Eventually, he turns into a parking lot and is jogging toward some shade trees at the end of the lot. I am a woman on a mission. I pull into the lot and follow him until he comes to rest. Then I roll down my window and cheerfully shout out—"I am a mom on a mission to keep people hydrated," and I hand him two bottles.

As I drive away, I glance in the mirror and see that he is drinking from one of the bottles and pouring water from the other one over his head.

A few days later I have the remaining water and granola bars in the back seat of my car as I drive downtown to peruse the farmers market with my friend Laurie. The market is near a highway overpass and frequently there are people who are homeless sitting on old wooden benches under the bridge. On my way out of the parking lot, I pull up to a red light and a man with a "homeless—please help" cardboard sign is walking toward my car. I open the window, call out to him, and offer up two bottles of water and a box of granola bars.

Glancing past him, I see that he has been sitting with friends under the bridge. So, I reach back for a six-pack of water and ask him to take it to his friends. As the light finally turns green, I drive away as four homeless people smile and wave at me.

Wes later tells me, "You infused the water with love and got to see the souls of all those people."

Future Self Revisited

In meditation with Wes in late August, we are once again exploring the energetic grid. If I imagine myself lying outstretched on the grid, I can see the earth below the openings in the grid, as though I am lying on a fishnet trampoline.

Today the grid is light-filled—sparkly—and there are a lot of spiritual orbs of light on the grid. In meditation, I interact with them and they appear fluid and joy filled. All light beings peer through the mesh to the earth below and can beam energy and light where needed to the people and places below. As I look through the mesh, I blow puffs of loving energy into friends on earth. There are layers and layers of the grid above me—expansive and sparkling.

As the meditation progresses, I encounter my future self, the highest most divine aspect of myself. She is an ascended angel— beautiful, light, and glowing. Her message to me is *Just share love everywhere. Do good things.*

There is more, and you will be shown.

My future self transports me to a beautiful monastery with many small apartments. Everyone meets in the courtyard. My friends and colleagues live there too. People come from all over to hear sermons, take classes, and gain inspiration. I wear simple clothing—flowing and beautiful. I am welcoming, loving, to my friends, and to those whom we serve.

In the evening, we have a ceremony to raise the earth's energy.

In meditation, I see that I am protected and held, and I am also my future self. Great waves of energy expand all around me. I see angels within the energy field. I am to bring stability, peace, and love to the planets and to support the lightworkers. I see all from here.

I have all I have ever needed. There is love, acceptance, joy, growth, and divine love for all.

Guardian

Inviting Irene to Spain

The following evening, I am struggling with meditation. I've been thinking about Irene and how much I miss her. I grab my journal to write.

COACH: You'll be fine—keep doing your work. Soon it will click in—you just want your brain to know how and when— but remember, enlightenment does not happen in the brain!

ME: Well, I miss my friend a lot lately. I know her spirit is here, but we used to have lots of fun and now she is not around.

COACH: Oh yes, she is! Sitting right next to you on your right side. See—she's getting you to smile. Irene sees all she wants to, and it makes her feel really good when you think of her. What do you want to know?

ME: Irene, I'm going to Spain in a few months to walk along the Camino Trail and I keep thinking of all the fun we had in Spain last time! Isn't it good that we didn't know about the cancer? I remember your headaches and all the Advil you took—what a trooper! That's what I've always admired about you—the stamina and how you were always engaging people and loving life! I know I rushed you sometimes—that was not about you being too slow—but about my own impatience. I am sorry.

I'd like you to be on the Camino Trail with me. I'll do all the exercise. You can come along for the ride. It will be so beautiful and charming in those small towns. I am so excited to break away from work for a while and just walk and think and be in nature.

Do you know how much you are missed, my friend? You brought so much joy and left us so quickly. In a meditation, I was opening up to light and filling up my body with it and suddenly I felt as though you and I were in *the La Sagrada Familia* in Barcelona and you were waving in the photo with the sun shining through the beautiful stained glass windows. How stunning was that place! And you were filled with love and light.

Please send me a sign that you are around. Goodnight, Irene.

A Sacred Gift

Time is passing quickly, and it is early September. The hot summer sun is beginning to cool earlier in the day.

Tonight, I experienced the most amazing of all meditations. After relaxing and settling in, I was guided to float above the earth and make myself as expansive as possible, focusing my energy in every direction. In this meditation, I was given a magnificent gift from the masters. The gift I received was a diamond-encrusted cross to shine light to others and attract those most in need of the light.

The commitment I made was to be that light. If I can stay in this elevated expanded place, everything is possible.

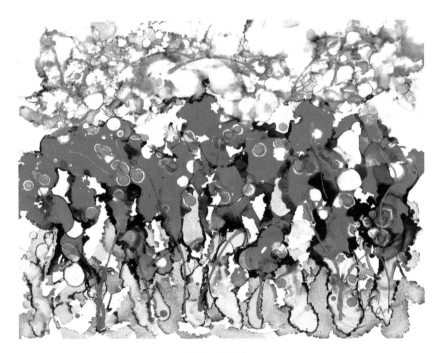

Going Within

Chapter 9

A Spiritual Journey Calls Me to Camino de Santiago—Fall

Taking My Quest Deeper on My Own

With Wes's guidance, I have been on an intensely introspective quest for months now, and it's time to take it to a deeper level on my own. I have learned to meditate while greatly reducing my internal chatter. I have attended retreats and experienced various spiritual practices. Now I am going to leave the country to walk the Camino de Santiago in Northern Spain. I give myself an A+ for my commitment to my 7 Personal Year journey.

Wes assures me, "If you continue to meditate you will have a deeper experience on the Camino Trail. Look for signs along the way and gather talismans to mark your journey."

I take his comments to heart, knowing that his messages to me are an important part of my progress. We will resume our meditation sessions in November.

The Camino de Santiago

I will begin walking the Camino de Santiago trail in Northern Spain in October and I am psyched! I will not have time to walk the entire 500-mile French Way but will walk 125 miles from the town of Ponferrada to Santiago de Compostela (Santiago). My journey will take nine days and I will celebrate in Santiago on the tenth day at the magnificent Santiago de Compostela Cathedral, one of the most important religious structures in all of Spain. It is believed that the cathedral holds the remains of St. Thomas the Apostle.

My adventurous and inspiring friend, Lory, will connect with me in Ponferrada after having already walked 375 miles of the trail over the previous month. We will walk together for several days and then meet another friend of ours, Becky, in Sarria to walk the remaining 60 miles together.

Rather than lugging backpacks and sleeping bags throughout the journey, we are taking a "Camino Lite" excursion. We'll carry only a daypack each day, and our accommodations and luggage transfers will be arranged through the small inns we stay at along the way. Every morning we must have our luggage in the lobby by 8:00 a.m. for it to be shuttled to our next destination.

I am excited, nervous, grateful, hesitant, awed, and on a very tight schedule to fly, travel by train, and bus to get to my first destination of León, where I will spend a day recuperating from jet lag before starting my journey. There is no wiggle room in the schedule. Everything possible has been planned and I must be on time.

This pilgrimage has been months in the planning, and I am filled with anticipation and trepidation. I have researched, shopped, re-shopped, packed, re-packed, and thrown out everything but the essentials. My boots are broken in. I have rain gear, sun gear, cool collapsible walking poles, and an I-can-do-this attitude.

I am envisioning exquisite scenery, lovely flat roads winding through the forest, farmland, and charming villages. I savor the idea of quiet reflection, deep spiritual insights, and new friendships.

I have romanticized the Camino as I am sure countless others have done over the thousands of years pilgrims have walked this trail. Yet I remember a cautionary text message from Lory just weeks ago saying, "Don't kid yourself … this is work!"

And so, the adventure begins.

The Train from Madrid to León

It is the end of September and I am exhausted from the long flight having left Minneapolis in the early evening, stopping first in Philadelphia, and then crossing the Atlantic Ocean. The morning sun streams through the windows of the airplane just a few hours after our evening departure from the US. I have never slept well in an upright position and I feel the stress and tension in myself and my fellow travelers as we do our best to endure the long flight.

When I arrive at the airport in Madrid, it is the hectic early morning commuting hours. I take a train from the airport to the train station, which is filled with travelers hurriedly crisscrossing the terminal, a buzzing hub of activity. I am instantly grateful that I will board a high-speed train with spacious, comfortable seating for my two-hour train ride to León. I can catch up on sleep and contemplate the journey that lies ahead.

As I wander through the terminal, stopping for a quick croissant and a café Americana, I attempt to decipher directions to the correct escalator that will bring me down one level to the waiting trains. Of course, the signs are all in Spanish. I realize instantly that my eight-week Beginning Spanish community education class is only helping me with the absolute essentials. I will have to remain on high alert to my surroundings to get where I need to go.

For instance, I believe I have found the correct departure train for León, so I enter a train car, stow my luggage, take a seat, and wait for the train to fill for the 10:00 a.m. departure. I am fifteen minutes early and the car is empty. Soon I notice that no one else is entering the train and it is getting dangerously near the time to depart. Suddenly, a harried train porter rushes through the train car rattling a message to me in Spanish with frantic hand signals that clearly indicate *Get off the train. Now!*

I have made a dire mistake with precious time to spare. I quickly grab my things, hop off the train, and bolt back to the station to get redirected to the correct train track. Thank God someone understands my ticket and points me in the right direction. I barely make it to my seat before the doors slam shut and the train accelerates out of the station. I have begun a long journey, and everything must fall perfectly into place. There is no room for error.

It is a no-nonsense crowd in my train car—quiet, reserved, engrossed in newspapers, books, nodding off to the gentle rhythm of the train. I am grateful to leave the city behind and enter a picturesque landscape of rolling hills and wide-open spaces. As the quiet train lulls my companions even further into their internal world, my mind drifts to my friend Irene and the wild train ride we took in England a few years back.

Irene and I toured England and Scotland for a self-guided ten days of adventure. On the final leg of our journey, we took a memorable two-hour train ride from Bath to London.

I grab my journal out of my backpack and I write:

ME: Irene, I knew you were with me on that long flight last night and I am thinking of you as I ride in this train this morning. Remember when we were on that crazy train ride from Bath to London? It was the last train of the day to London after our long Sunday of touring Bath in the sweltering heat. The train car was packed, and the crowd was exhausted from the weekend and in need of a restful quiet time. We ended up sitting a few rows apart from each other because it was so crowded.

There was that one extremely large, loud, and obnoxious woman filling the train with tales that no one was interested in hearing. Do you remember? She was in the center of the train car seated at a table where the seats faced each other. While she rambled on from one loud story to the next, her tablemates looked bored, worn out, and yet made no effort to stop her, perhaps realizing that it would be to no avail.

Eventually, from a remote section of the train, a big bully of a guy leaped up out of his seat and, with his face puffed up and red, shouted to her, "STOP TALKING!" Dead silence settled over the crowd. Not one person jumped to her defense—she had, after all, claimed all the space in that train car through her brash, animated bantering. It was so awkward, and we were collectively stunned into silence.

The accused, with a look of defiance on her face, ignored him and continued her incessant chatter. And that is when he just lost it! As his voice lunged at her, he roared, "You are an ugly fat pig! You disgust me! You disgust everyone! SHUT UP!"

And again, there was that deafening silence before you dared to turn your head ever so slowly and glance back at me. With that one look at each other, we burst into uncontrollable and utterly silent laughter. So intense were our emotions and the laughter we were holding onto that we could hardly breathe. Schoolgirls being reprimanded—desperate to stifle our inappropriate response.

My friend, did you know on some level, even then, that it would soon be your time to leave?

IRENE: Not really—but once I passed, I saw that it had been in my plan.

ME: You should see how beautiful it is heading north. No more North Dakota prairie land. It's hilly, the mountains are coming, and I'm going to be walking them!

IRENE: Ugh—you're crazy. I'd never do it. But, this time I can fly so I might come along.

ME: It's kind of surreal here. I know you are right here. You made such a fast departure. I will be thinking about you on the trail during hours and hours of walking. Just thinking about it is exhausting me. Time for a little nap.

Lost and Found in León

A few hours later, the train slows to a halt. Glancing out the window, I see that the station sign does not indicate that we have arrived in León. Believing that there are a few other stops to make before reaching our destination, I take my time watching others gather their bags and depart the train.

The car empties quickly and I think it's strange that so many are exiting at this station toting backpacks and hiking sticks. That's when I finally ask a porter walking by if this is the León station. He snaps to attention! Wide-eyed with a panicked look on his face, he frantically rushes me and my luggage off the train just before the door slams shut! Suddenly I know I was seconds away from being trapped on the train as it reversed directions to zip back to Madrid. Disaster averted!

My guidebook assures me that it is a close "10-minute walk" from the train station to my hotel located in old town. The first train station agents I encounter do not speak English, nor do I speak Spanish, so they cannot understand my quizzical expressions or the map I am holding. I attempt to converse with a few other agents, and, with puzzled expressions, they vaguely point in the direction of a cathedral across the river. I decide to forge ahead and do my best to find the hotel on my own.

As I exit the station, I am grateful to be standing on solid ground. Though the day is heating up and I am exhausted, I know a hot shower awaits me. I am content.

Two hours later, my patience has run dry. None of the street names align with the map—plus they are written in Spanish so are difficult to find. Streets appear to run off in every direction and I am in tangle town. From time to time, I stop in a town square and sit on a lone park bench for a welcome rest, resigning myself to the fact that I am getting nowhere. Even holding my map and looking confused has not attracted any attention. It appears no one speaks English.

Finally, I must look pitiful enough, because an English-speaking Spanish woman asks me if I am lost. She studies my map and seems to be just as confused as I am about the whereabouts of my hotel. It appears that I must now follow the fortress wall for several blocks, cross the busy intersection, and walk around the park and the perimeter of a large museum. Then I will encounter a side street across from the *only* shopping center—and my hotel *should* be at the end of that street. I have no idea if I am even understanding her correctly.

I graciously thank her and start walking in the direction of the mythical hotel, lugging my overnight bag behind me—daypack on my back. After a tiring fifteen-minute walk, I finally see a sign above a small hotel at the end of a quiet side street. I am beyond grateful. I cannot wait for a quick shower and a long nap.

I trudge to the hotel entrance and notice that all the glass is darkened a smoky color, so I am unable to see the interior. Is this a cruel trick? Is this hotel out of business? This can't be the entrance. So certain am I, that I don't even try the door.

My next brilliant thought is that they must have moved the entrance to the side of the building. It is irrational, but I am a desperate woman, and I just want to get to my room. I drag myself around the corner, glance up, and across the street, directly behind the hotel, there is a gigantic sign that says "**IRENNE**" perched on top of a storefront.

Unbelievable! This is impossible. If I had not walked around the corner and looked up, I would have never seen the sign I asked for. Now I know for certain that Irene is on this journey with me.

With a surge of energy and a beaming smile on my face, I return to the front of the hotel and enter the smoky glass doors to check in. Later, in my room, I take the long-awaited, steaming shower and then fall into a deep dreamless sleep for the rest of the day and night.

Storefront behind the hotel

Sunday in León—Wandering through Old Town

Sunday morning, I awake early to the sun streaming through the shuttered windows I have left open throughout the night. It is a warm autumn day and I am well-rested and up for anything the day might bring.

After a leisurely breakfast of rich expresso and a delicious almond croissant, I stroll down the narrow street that leads me past small shops and cafes, and through a centuries-old stone archway into the old town. As I wander through old town, I enter the side door of the first cathedral I see, the Basilica de San Isidoro. I am alone in the darkened sanctuary and sit quietly close to the altar. As relaxation settles over me, I silently talk with Irene about some favorite memories of our trip to Spain last fall. As I am thinking of her, I feel the familiar pressure on top of my head and am grateful for her presence. I feel her warmth as she sits next to me and it is as though we are back together in the cathedrals of Barcelona and Madrid.

I spend a few hours strolling through the expansive open-air market. It's Sunday and families with their young children are everywhere. Linked arm-in-arm, adults peruse the many vendor stands of fresh fruits and vegetables, meats and cheeses, and a variety of local crafts. Meanwhile, the children run wild, darting about and chasing each other through the cobblestone streets. The shrieks and laughter of children are everywhere.

In the early evening, after a quick nap back at the hotel, I return to old town and find a charming, quaint tavern along a quiet street near the cathedral. I sit at one of the few outside tables along the street, order a beer, and pull out my map and journal to capture my thoughts as I admire the good-looking Spaniards strolling by on the steep and winding street.

I'm having a hard time focusing on my map and journal. There is so much distraction. For instance, there are so many dogs wandering by, yet none of them is barking. Are there some rules the dogs are aware of that keep them in line?

And now, I notice the most amazing shoes and boots walking by on the locals. Plus, black tights. Leather jackets. (Okay, I wouldn't mind being back in my twenties with these cute guys walking by.)

I take a sip of beer and begin to write with Coach.

Relaxing in León

COACH: What is the significance of being here?

ME: I have been here—long ago in another time. These winding streets feel like home … family, friendship, closeness. I feel nostalgic for another time. My loved ones were here, too. I feel like Jess and Matt (my daughter and her boyfriend) could walk by at any moment. Wouldn't that be great? Loves of my life.

COACH: Well, people want to be acknowledged—smiled at. They might not reciprocate. That's okay—it's how you reach their soul.

Have you thought about the walk? Do you know why we arranged it?

ME: Irene? To remember our eternal connection? (Honestly, there goes another pair of the most darling dress boots!)

COACH: Okay, back to business. You will be guided on the trail. We are sending in the troops to be with you. It's an indoctrination—you are walking the Way of St. James. A familiar road for you. Watch for signs—it's an adventure and a huge time to reflect. You miss your friend, Irene, who understands the draw Europe has for you. You've been her sister for a long time—glued at the hip.

We're sorry it was her time so soon, but there's a bigger plan. Plus, she's up to lots of heavy work on this side—work she loves, of course.

Did you know she is an angel to many people—working past human personalities, right to the heart?

ME: I do know, and I am in awe. Irene, do you remember the day we were ridiculously hungry in Madrid and we couldn't figure out how to read the menu, so we saw a picture of a steak dinner posted on the outer wall of a restaurant and sat right down at the outside patio? We were beyond exhausted until they brought the complimentary liquor—which was fabulous—followed by a few heavenly glasses of wine. And though we look terrible in the photos, we had an outstanding time—one of our best memories.

I've been tearful off and on today. There is a weird dichotomy. I miss your human companionship, but in a way, I feel closer and more connected with you now that you are on the other side.

COACH: Remember what Wes said about gathering a talisman for the journey. And be sure to ponder questions along the way.

ME: Commercial break—look at this fashion parade strolling by! The scarves here are fantastic as are the golden-toned saddle shoes.

Then there are the occasional high heels. What? High heels make no sense on cobblestone streets, but they are chic, nonetheless. Even the guys have scarves around their necks—so cool.

Here comes a guy in rose red pants. Wow! But it looks right here.

And now a mother and daughter walk by arm in arm. Love that!

And here is a couple walking hand in hand (note to self: my next guy is going to show some romantic moves).

No one is following the guidance about no white pants or white purses after September first. Ha!

A big look for the boys is closely cropped hair with curls on top. And sneakers with tight pants to top off the look.

The dogs here are ridiculously cute. (I take another swig of beer.)

The tourists are easily spotted in sensible attire … ill-fitting sweatshirts and sensible shoes. (I PRAY I do not look like that!)

Now a sweet grandma walks by linked arm in arm with her handsome son. He is smiling my way, knowing clearly that he is a chick magnet by treating his mother well.

By the way ... where is the waiter? Is there a one-beer rule here?

Okay—I do love a great suede jacket and camel-colored scarf. (Note to self—a form-fitted puffy vest is great with a neck scarf.)

And why are some still wearing sunglasses? The sun went down an hour ago!

Also, a work-type blazer is a fashion kill. Ditto to crewneck sweatshirts on females. No tight flowered legging—EVER—even if I am as thin as Katey Sagal when she was Peg Bundy in *Married... with Children*!

Here comes my first charcoal tam on an extremely cute Spanish guy. He's with his fashionable wife.

A man pushing a baby stroller is also a chick magnet. That guy does direct eye to eye with me.

Now, there is a guy with a palm tree on his t-shirt. It looks a bit off but is forgiven for his good looks.

I love the Spanish language. So beautiful, but I must work on rolling my *r*'s.

Tonight, I will sleep well, and tomorrow I'll take a bus to Ponferrada where I will meet up with Lory to begin the real journey.

I surrender to no more journaling today. I need to get back to the hotel for a good night of sleep and then head to the bus station in the morning to begin my journey.

Day 1—One Foot in Front of the Other

Ponferrada to Villafranca del Bierzo—Fourteen Miles

I awake in a strange bed in a strange town and I am on edge. My friend Lory says, "It's just walking." But I am keyed up. It's silly, but I want to do this right. My last big hike in Europe was years ago when I was in my early twenties. I was carefree, in shorts and sandals, lugging my backpack in and out of trains as I made my way via Eurail Pass through several countries. I was light and carefree with no pain in my body and no expectations other than to live right in the moment.

Now I want to do this right. I am older, wiser, and I know all about blisters, fatigue, and arthritis. I have created a compelling vision of myself decked out in the perfect hiking attire. After months of careful planning. I've tried on every boot in my hometown, found collapsible hiking poles, and have the best blister-proof socks made.

I've read the blogs and watched the movie *The Way* twice. Yet, I know my efforts have only prepared me for the first day of my journey. I have heard that college graduation only prepares you for the first day of your new job—all the learning comes after that. So it is with the Camino.

I am *off to school*, standing at the bus stop anticipating the first day. Only this is not school. It is a path, and the path is filled with the souls of those who have already walked for hundreds of miles for thousands of years to Santiago. It is a path that is breathtakingly beautiful and at times treacherous and unrelenting.

Those who have already walked 375 miles across northern Spain, starting at St. Jean Pied de Port are the juniors and seniors. I am an incoming freshman, desperate to blend into the flow but uncertain of my capabilities.

Years ago, I had a vivid dream in which I was hiking up a steep mountain path and had fallen into a ravine. Two hikers were walking the same path and as they passed me deep in conversation, the older man reached down and grabbed my arm to help me up and back onto the trail. Not a word was spoken as they continued along their way.

That is the Camino. Everyone is on the path. There is help and guidance when needed—but each walks the path in his or her own way. I must ask for help when I need it.

Now I will be on the path and my friend will be showing me the ropes. In a local pub last evening, a group of seasoned pilgrims declared that it will be "an easy day"—only fourteen miles with not too many ups and downs. The guidebook suggests it can be walked in six hours. Lory and her new Camino friends, Jan from Oregon, and Greg and Joe from Illinois, are drinking a beer and confidently looking forward to the next day's adventure.

At 8:00 a.m. the following morning, after a quick breakfast of hard rolls, meats, and cheeses, Lory and I begin our day's journey and I quickly feel a rhythm set in. We are walking and chatting and occasionally tossing a *"Buen Camino"* to our fellow travelers. We walk through parks, along a beautiful river, on dirt paths through grape-filled farmlands. I am thinking … okay, I am doing this. I can keep up with my energetic friend and we will be at our destination by mid-afternoon to enjoy a leisurely stroll around town with a nice hearty dinner and some Spanish wine.

Hours roll by and by mid-afternoon, I am beginning to crave an end to this walk—but we've miles to go and much of it is traversing the hilly countryside. I stop when I can to take photographs and must admit to myself that most photos will be taken when I've reached my limit and need to stop to breathe and lean on my poles for support.

As the afternoon drags on, Lory and I walk through a creepy abandoned town that seems to accentuate the self-doubt and remorse I am feeling. This is not quite what I imagined. We quickly walk through it and are back again in the rolling farmland that we must conquer before we reach our village.

Now, I am slowing way down. My feet shuffle. My legs are wobbling, weak, and no longer want to support me. Lory, a graceful flamingo from her month of walking, is ahead of me now and is full of drive and energy from her time on the trail. I stop several times on the slightest inclines and feel lightheaded and exhausted.

I have a two-liter water pack on my back and have used it from time to time for hydration whenever I think about it. I am soon to learn that my effort is too small, and I am seriously dehydrated.

We finally arrive at our destination as evening settles in behind the drizzling grey clouds. It has been nine hours of walking with few breaks, not the six hours the guidebook suggests. It is a quaint old town: cobblestone streets with steep inclines and bad building markers. Our guidebook map is useless. I am so exhausted I can

Camino signs pointing the way

only lean against the brick wall of an old building as Lory sprints down the cobblestoned street, in cold, drizzling rain, to find our hotel. I lean on my poles, depleted, and resigned. I am literally standing still, so exhausted I cannot put one foot in front of the next. I am hot, sweaty, and chilled to the bone.

We check into an old village inn with dark, low wooden ceilings and thick grey stone walls. It looks like it has been here hundreds of years. I pull myself slowly up the steep stairs, luggage in hand, and when I get to my room I begin shaking uncontrollably. I quickly pull the water bladder out of my backpack and realize, with horror, that I have only consumed a third of the water and we have walked for hours! Instantly, I pour glass after glass of water into myself, stand under a pulsing hot shower massage, and collapse into bed for a two-hour crash. I must be rested for tomorrow.

Day 2—Climbing to New Heights

Villafranca del Bierzo to O Cebreiro — Seventeen miles

The guidebook warns us: this day we must be mentally prepared. It's going to be a long, arduous journey ending in a four-kilometer meandering walk up the mountain, to arrive at the remote mountaintop village of O Cebreiro. Our guidebook suggests we will be walking for ten hours. (I am suspicious that it will be midnight before I arrive). Fellow pilgrims who have walked the trail in the past say it is one of the toughest legs of the journey.

At dinner the prior evening, Lory confesses to me that on our first day of walking together, she walked at a much slower pace than she is used to. I do not hesitate to tell her, "Walk at your own pace. I will be behind you. It's okay, I want time for reflection."

This is only a half-truth. Yes, I want to reflect and travel solo. But Lory is a fun companion and I yearn to keep up her pace and banter throughout the day while crossing the magnificent countryside with the endlessly entertaining stream of fellow pilgrims passing by.

The minute I tell her to walk ahead, I am flooded with relief. I can stop as often as I want on the inclines, lean on my poles, and catch my breath. Maybe shoot a photo or two. Besides, she wants to challenge herself and take the route that goes up and over a steep hill and through the forest. I prefer the flatter, gentler path along the country road and in the woods.

We wake to a beautiful morning, grab a quick breakfast of hard rolls, meats, cheeses, and strong coffee, and step outside to a cool, fall day. We immediately start walking up a steep incline to exit the town and I am already catching my breath while the experienced pilgrims don't seem to be expending any effort. Soon I am lagging behind, walking alone along a winding brook that follows the road through the mountains. It is a stunning path to walk and I don't even mind the small groups and solo hikers passing me by. I have settled into this journey and appreciate the time alone.

In the small towns and hamlets that appear every three or four miles, fellow pilgrims are taking short breaks. There is a sense of urgency, though some will stop at the fourteen-mile mark and tackle the mountain in the morning. I imagine that most hikers are thinking of the steep winding incline up that mountain and want to arrive at the final destination before dark.

I vacillate between seeing this as the best experience of my life and plunging into feelings of despair. In these dark moments, I yearn for companionship—but today that is not an option.

There are signs along the way: "Rent horses here to get up the mountain!" I think of the three fellow travelers, Joe, Greg, and Jan, that Lory has become friends with along the way. Last night as we played a few rounds of Yahtzee at a local pub, Lory shared with them that she has been dreaming of riding a horse up the mountain. They think it's a great idea and decide to check it out too.

I overhear someone on the path mentioning taking a taxicab up the mountain and I begin justifying that decision for myself. Am I guilty of backing out of my one hundred percent commitment to walking this entire 125 miles? I want the satisfaction of doing it all, but I also do not relish trudging up a steep mountain exhausted in the dark. Besides, I do not see taxi stands anywhere—maybe someone made that up.

I've been walking for hours now and I am slowing way down. The mountain ahead weighs heavily in my mind and I know that I will not make it by nightfall. I am tense, wondering what I should do. How will I get to my destination? I pass pilgrims on horses being led in small groups, and many others plow ahead on foot—now the light banter has been replaced by intense focus and silence.

I think, maybe if I could have climbed this mountain in the morning it would be no big deal. But now I am so tired, and I just want to get to O Cebreiro.

A miracle occurs in the last dusty old town at the base of the mountain. I am at the fourteen-mile mark and the afternoon sun is beginning to fade when I stumble upon a bar and restaurant with a huge Taxi Stop sign. I am overwhelmed with gratitude as I point to the sign and furiously nod yes to the bartender!

Once I am safely in a cab, I find that the Spanish taxi driver does not speak a word of English and it is a thirty-minute cab ride up the pocked, gravel mountain road meandering up to O Cebreiro. We are conversing most of the way up the mountain in languages neither of us understands. It doesn't matter—he knows where I am headed, and I know he has transported many equally exhausted pilgrims.

As we continue up the steep incline, we pass pilgrims on horses and even the horses look exhausted. Others are in cabs. Those that are walking look humorless, hot, determined … refugees trudging up the mountain in a staggered line.

From time to time, my cab driver slows down and gestures to me. Do I want to take a photo of the incredible landscape down the mountain? I am blown away by the breathtaking view, but I have no interest in stopping—I simply do not want to stand up.

I feel guilty that I have taken the shortcut—the easy way out. This is not the me I try to be in daily life. Yet, I know it would not be humanly possible for me to walk the entire journey up the mountain before dark. Is this what it means to ask for help when one needs it? Could this possibly be a sign of strength?

The taxi driver drops me off at the edge of the tiny village—a cluster of centuries-old stone buildings. It is freezing cold in this mountain village and I have no idea where my friends are. Which of these five small inns holds my luggage? Why did I fail to record in which inn I'd be staying? I silently chastise myself.

After I have wandered about and rested on benches outside of the few shops for an hour or so, my friends finally arrive. As it turns out, Joe and Greg made reservations last night for horse rides up the mountain (a choppy, treacherous two-hour ride). All reservations were taken by morning, so Lory and Jan started up the mountain and finally surrendered to hail a cab after being passed on the trail by someone being pushed in a wheelchair by a group of friends.

Suddenly everything is okay again. I made it. I can rest now. I am not the loser pilgrim I thought myself to be. I am not lost in the dark. Not everyone can walk this trail perfectly, but I am doing my best.

Fit and healthy pilgrims arrive in a steady stream of small groups—they appear to have effortlessly made the hike up the mountain. Perhaps they have come from countries where mountain hiking is the norm. Places like Switzerland, Austria, Germany. They seem refreshed and exhilarated.

We settle in for dinner in our charming inn with the roaring brick fireplace, as cold, steady rain falls and the fog rolls in.

Day 3—What Goes Up Must Come Down

O Cebreiro to Triacastela—Fourteen Miles

The next morning, we wake at dawn to a thick fog and the same gentle steady rain from the evening before. It's been raining all night with no hint of stopping anytime soon. It will be a challenging journey downhill via slippery rocks, limited visibility, uncertain footing. Greg and Joe have decided to bypass the walk and cab it to the next town to avoid falling off cliffs or breaking a leg.

Lory, Jan, and I are committed to walking and I admit to myself that I am nervous. It will be easy to get separated in the fog, especially if I am unable to keep up with my friends. They are used to gracefully traversing the steep declines; I am not.

We stay close through most of the journey. Even though we are walking down the mountain, we have plenty of opportunity to go up sudden inclines. We are in hiking gear, raincoats, rain hats, and ponchos. Should we take a sudden fall, our clothing will protect us from breaking any bones. Occasionally I lose track of my partners and I can actually look around and take a deep breath. It is beyond beautiful yet the drive to keep up the pace takes me away from these moments of splendor.

The rain is steady, and we trudge on in our ponchos—bright spots on a grey soggy day. I am thinking that fourteen miles downhill can be completed in no time, but I have failed to factor in all the starts and stops of traversing on slippery rocks and trails.

There are plenty of beautiful landscapes, but no one is really interested. We are on a mission that involves one hundred percent vigilance. After a quick sandwich and coffee at a roadside stop, we continue slogging through the rain. The path provides plenty of challenges and by mid-afternoon leads us to a small bar just a mile or two short of our final descent. This section has been highlighted on the guidebook map as being particularly steep and challenging. It looks like a drop-off to me.

I decide then and there that I will not complete the final leg of this journey. I am simply too exhausted and tense. I believe I will not be able to accomplish it without imminent peril. I am once again drained, and in no mood for slippery declines and uncertain turns on the path. The rain is coming down harder now and the mountain is a grey cloud of choking fog.

Lory and Jan decide to continue walking after assuring me they will see me soon. They are not to be deterred by lousy weather and perceived threats. They have already successfully navigated so many challenges on their journey since Saint Jean Pied-de-Port that they are not about to give up now.

I am alone in the small tavern with only one bartender and someone attending to dirty glassware. A television high on a wall shows an intense soccer game being broadcast in Spanish. A cab has been called and I sit and wait in silence. I am left to my thoughts and my very small self. When did I get so cowardly? If this cozy bar were not here, I would have been forced to keep going. I could have asked my friends for help and support, but I keep forgetting to think that way—not wanting to be a burden. What is the lesson here?

Suddenly I recall participating in a ropes course exercise in a leadership developing program I attended years ago. We were a group of eighteen plus two leaders, climbing trees in the redwood forests in Northern California. Each of us, one by one, was challenged to climb a tall pole and walk across on a rope extended from tree to tree. I was terrified and waited until the very end to climb the pole just as the sun was beginning to set.

At the urging of the leaders, we were told to ask the group below us for whatever help we needed. Most shouted out a desire for words of encouragement, assurances that they could make it. I shouted down that I wanted them to sing to me, and with

Christmas carols floating up to me one after the other, I courageously inched my way across the rope to the other side.

Now I sit waiting for a cab to arrive, thinking that I could have walked to my destination instead of waiting. This is my penalty for wimping out—and I am not proud. I have plenty of time to reflect.

Later I hear that the path wasn't so bad after all. It seems you can't always trust the guidebook. The winding path descent looks treacherous, but it is an easy trip down. We settle in for a night of dining, drinking, and games with our fellow pilgrims.

Miles of winding roads

Day 4—I'll Take the High Road, You'll Take the Low Road

Triacastela to Sarria—Twelve Miles

There are two options today. One is shorter but ascends rapidly into the mountains. The other is longer and descends to a monastery before reaching the next town.

I take the high road, and Lory and Jan take the low road. It is the first day that I am completely on my own. I can let go of my incessant comparison of my slow pace with their confident, quick strides.

I start up the trail and keep waiting for the steep mountain path, but it never appears. Maybe I am adjusted to hiking enough that I do not lament each time I round a bend and see the trail inclining. It is just a long, slowly winding road that continues to ascend, but at a reasonable pace. I am delighted.

The scenery takes my breath away and I feel strong and capable. The ups and downs are challenging, yet interesting too. The path is at times wide, flat, and stone-free; at other times it is filled with large slanted rocks, loose pebble, and deep ruts. This day is mostly the latter, but my good walking sticks and freedom from self-doubt keep me grounded on the path.

I must stay vigilant, and from time to time I remind myself to stop and look around. This is paradise. The air is sweet with the smells of fresh woods and the colors and sounds are spectacular. I thank God for this opportunity.

In a tiny hamlet in the middle of nowhere, I walk around the corner of an old stone cottage and stumble upon a small gathering. It is a mini-Woodstock, with lots of chatter, people meditating on an oriental rug, pilgrims lounging on a few badly worn couches and lawn chairs, and a canopy over everyone. There is plenty of food and beverages "by donation only." I see how people share and engage, and know that this is what the good life is really about—camaraderie, support, love. It's enough to keep me uplifted when it is time to move along.

As I hike through the beautiful countryside, I have hours to think about whatever I want or about nothing at all. I think about Irene and how she would love it here—though such a long journey on foot would never have been her cup of tea. I am glad she is near me in spirit so that she can also enjoy this magnificent countryside.

Late in the afternoon, all of us arrive at once to the outskirts of Sarria and it is a long walk into town to our hotel. Sarria is a picturesque town with a charming, winding river walk. After a quick happy hour, we cross the old stone bridge and find a quaint pizza parlor in old town for dinner. Tomorrow is our first day walking with our newest pilgrim friend, Becky, who has just arrived from back home in Minnesota. She is a breath of fresh air! Upbeat, engaging, and all ready for the journey.

Day 5 Meltdown—A Hit-the-Wall Day

Sarria to Portomarin—Fifteen Miles

My alarm goes off and I am instantly filled with dread. I am exhausted. Overnight my legs have turned to Lincoln Logs and will not bend. Somehow, I find the strength to crawl out of bed and stuff myself back into full regalia—two pairs of socks, boots, three layers of t-shirts that can easily be pulled off when the sun is high in the sky. Jacket, hat, sunglasses, lip balm, sunscreen, foot bandages, and daypack loaded with rain jacket, map, and guidebook.

We begin our daily journey as a small team and in no time, Lory, Jan, and now Becky, are out of sight (brisk steps, strong legs, laughter filling the air). I walk in solitude, my preferred way now since I cannot keep up with my friends. I admit it's discouraging, but I quickly set those thoughts aside. Today, I need all the energy I can muster.

I think about Irene—as I have most days when I am not preoccupied with keeping alert on the path. I wonder how she is doing, what I need to know from the other side, when she will appear again.

Last night, I read a blog written by my friend Art who is a close friend from years ago. His blog was about his terminal lung disease and his daily mantra: *Slow down by half, then half again; enjoy life twice as much.* He is looking toward the end of his life and is sharing great wisdom with us. He does not have much time left.

Two friends gone—lung diseases and early deaths—and I am in dismay about walking fourteen miles? It's time to toughen up!

My body is so sore, and by mid-morning I am totally disheartened. I stop for a quick coffee at an outdoor cafe just outside a small village. Sitting at the tiny aluminum table in the hot sun, I drink my rich dark coffee while feeling intense sadness for the loss of my friends.

After some time, I know I must continue my journey, so I hoist on my pack, grab my poles, and hit the trail once again, feeling deeply solemn and reflective.

I am just past the coffee stop on my way to the next village when I pass through a small hamlet with a few old buildings surrounding it. Out of the corner of my eye, I catch a glimpse of an old man, tucked behind some trees next to an old wooden shack. He is sitting on a tree stump intently whittling a walking stick. When he looks up, I murmur a polite *"Hola"* in his direction as I quickly walk by. Suddenly he motions intensely for me to come over to him. I toss a casual "No, no" his way and keep walking. Now he shouts, "Bella! Bella!" so I decide to turn around and go behind the bushes to see what he wants.

In rapid Spanish, this gentle old man with exactly one tooth (I counted), a stooped-over body, bald head, and magnificent grey eyes takes my hand and gently places a walnut in my palm. He is trying to tell me something with great intensity and the only word I comprehend is *"Santiago."*

I nod my head vigorously, "Yes, yes, Santiago!" and he reaches into his pocket and places two more walnuts into my palm.

What does this mean? Are these a blessing for my travels? A wish for good luck? A message he wants me to deliver in Santiago?

He smiles and nods at me, watching me with twinkling grey eyes as I back away, blowing a kiss to him, and putting the precious walnuts into my pocket. I am warmed by his caring; it is a moment of pure grace and compassion.

I am back walking on the path for only a moment when unexpected tears well up inside me. I think of this old man's kindness and then I think of how my friend Art will be dying soon and I realize that what he has written is true. Only when we slow way down can we see the true kindness of strangers and friends.

Alone on this path, in the middle of nowhere, I finally feel that I can let down my guard and cry out loud. In a torrent of tears, I release all the pent-up grief for the loss of my friend Irene and now for my good friend Art whose profound words have touched me deeply.

I silently tell Irene that I am so sorry I have not cried more for her passing. *I am so sad and miss our friendship and all the fun we had.* I grieve for all we will not experience now that she is no longer on earth.

As I walk, I think of all this with intense sadness. I spiral deeper into feeling of inadequacies about not being able to keep up on this journey. Never mind that my feet and legs are killing me.

A minute later, I round a bend and see that in fifty yards or so I will be walking right by a farmer who is standing on a ladder, collecting walnuts from a tree just off the path. I am mortified that he might have heard me sobbing, and now know that I must contain myself. My eyes are no doubt swollen and red, but I think I can quickly pass by him with my eyes to the ground murmuring a quick "*Hola.*"

I stifle my tears and just as I am a few feet from him, a walnut falls on the path directly in front of me. It is a moment of decision. Without thinking, I quickly scoop up the walnut and hold it up to him. He looks me straight in the eyes, smiles at me, and blows me two kisses. It is a stunning moment. He knows that I am deeply saddened, and he is an angel offering his support and a glimpse of his soul.

I quickly move along and now I am finally around the corner on my way out of the hamlet when I see that someone has drawn a large heart in the sand right in the middle of the path. I place the three chestnuts in the heart, snap a photo, and just like that I am comforted and calmed. A great cloud has lifted.

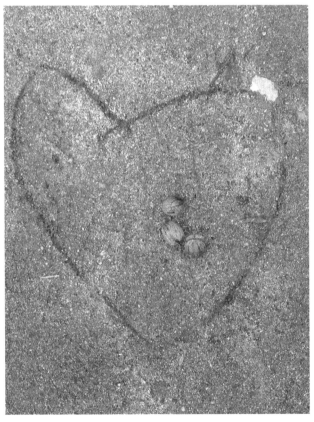

Inspiration for the journey

Hours later, I descend into the village of Portomarin. I have viewed it from a long way away, and it seems like it has taken forever to arrive. I yearn to take off my hiking boots and settle in for a restful evening.

At the edge of town, I come to a long, deep, and slippery ravine—the worst I have seen so far on this journey. Every step must be taken with great caution—sideways moves with poles guiding each step. The descent requires full concentration, courage, stamina, perfect foot placement. I am tense as I descend down the steep ravine and then confident and full of gratitude as I reach the bottom of the passage.

When I finally arrive at my hotel, weak and exhausted, I find that my friends are all booked into another hotel on the other side of town. I will spend this chilly, rainy evening alone settled in my own cozy inn.

As it turns out, it's a magical evening. I dine with two couples walking the trail together; I encountered them earlier in the day. They are deeply spiritual people who met at church years ago and remain married to this day. They ask me difficult questions: "What are your spiritual beliefs?" and "Who are you?"

I am struck by their openness to share themselves. The men are good looking and appear to adore their wives, getting up to grab them a fresh napkin, or serving them first at the table. I notice that the admiration is mutual, and the women treat their spouses with great respect.

I ponder whether I am ready to open up to a man in my life once again. As the evening goes on, I find myself sharing more about what is happening in my life, about my friend Irene, and how walking this trail is impacting me in so many ways. These are good people and I feel so much better about things now, after our deep conversation.

Day 6—Up And Over

Portomarin to Palas de Rei—Fifteen Miles

I awake early in the morning and pure joy replaces all despair from yesterday. There is just one more steep hill to ascend right on the outskirts of town and then it will be downhill all the way to Santiago. At least that is what it looks like from the elevation map in the guidebook.

My fellow travelers and I plan to meet at the town center just after sunrise to get a good start on the day. When they haven't arrived thirty minutes after our arranged meeting time, I start walking. The cobbled street leads to the edge of town, then over an old stone arch bridge, and straight up a long ascent on the path.

With each step, I remind myself that once I get to the top it will be all downhill. There will be occasional inclines, but the bulk of the work is now over—I think. I am thrilled.

It seems like the incline goes on and on, and everyone is relying on walking sticks to help them ascend. I stop from time to time to catch my breath and take in the view. When I view the incline from the peak, I see that every piece of the Camino trail is really stunning.

Mid-morning, I stop for a quick cup of coffee at a rest stop along the side of the road. Just as I am wondering if I will ever catch up to my friends, I suddenly see them coming up the trail toward me. Immense gratitude fills me. For once, I am the one ahead on the journey! Apparently, they got a late start, after all, so they will stop here while I move ahead down the trail.

I meander along throughout the afternoon. It's a winding trail through the countryside and I am in solitude most of the day. More and more I am finding great companionship in silence. It is then that I pause to really look at my beautiful surroundings. I am so grateful to be here on this trail and I always feel like Irene is right beside me.

Day 7—The Town that Never Ends

Palas de Rei to Arzua—Seventeen Miles

Today is a seventeen-mile walk to Arzua, a larger city than the ones we have stayed in along the way. The trail is more level than I have experienced in the past few days, and yet it is an arduous journey with hours of solitary hiking through the countryside.

All roads lead to Santiago

There is plenty of time to ponder as I walk, one pole in front of the other down the narrow lanes, over bridges and through miles of rolling farmland. I vacillate between thinking this journey is the best thing I have ever done in my life and wondering when I will finally arrive at the ultimate destination.

I silently chastise myself. *Why is it so challenging to stay present in the moment, accepting what is, and finding joy here?*

The afternoon passes uneventfully and by early evening I finally arrive at the edge of town, only to realize that my hotel is still a good three-mile hike to the other end of town. I am truly exhausted.

When I finally arrive at the hotel, and after a quick shower, I drag myself into the dining room where I meet up with my companions. Becky reports that we have walked 47,000 steps today! An amazing record for all of us.

Day 8—Stops and Starts

Arzua to O Amenal—Fourteen Miles

This is an odd day. The distance is shorter than on some of the other days, but the walk through the winding countryside seems to go on and on.

Once again, my friends have gone on ahead and I am walking at my own pace, passing small hamlets along the way. Since breakfasts are minimal at the hotels, I am anticipating lunch and checking the guidebook to see where my next meal is coming from.

It seems that hours go by walking through fields and small villages, and it is mid-afternoon when I finally see a roadside bar and restaurant—a heavenly sight for a weary pilgrim. It's a rustic place with an overdose of potted plants and a thick wooden bar counter with carvings decades old.

I was hoping to grab a sandwich and be back on the trail, but I see that my only option is to seat myself at a small table and order off the menu. Behind me, a couple is enjoying fresh, hearty bread, a lovely merlot, and a beautiful steaming pasta dish with chicken and thick marinara. I am ravenous.

Across from me, a table of four is enjoying a leisurely lunch of pork chops, fries, and a crisp vegetable salad laced in oil and vinaigrette. Wine and bread of course.

The waiter arrives at my table in a whirl. He is the proprietor and waiter—and he is very rushed since many patrons at the bar are waiting for service and he is short-staffed. He speaks zero English.

As he describes the specials in great detail, I shake my head and say, *"Yo no hablo español!"* several times until he is reduced to simple hand gestures.

He points to the pasta behind me and I vigorously nod my head, "Yes, yes!" He points to the pork chops on the table beside me and I rub my stomach and say "Yum!" a big smile on my face. He says, *"Ensalada?"* I nod enthusiastically, and then he whisks away just as I am about to tell him that I will take the pork chops.

Soon my table is laden with thick, crusty bread, olive oil, and a deep red wine. I am in heaven. The pasta arrives and I dig in. It is delicious and I make it through about half of the dish before I am stuffed.

It's time for me to go. Now, where is the waiter? I need my check because I must be on my way. I still have many miles to walk according to the guidebook, and I need to make it to the next hotel before dark.

I rise from the table just as my waiter breezes through the kitchen swing door with a platter of two sizzling pork chops and a pile of fries.

I gasp!

My stunned look causes my neighboring diners to burst into laughter, pointing at the new dish that is arriving. Once again, I curse my inability to grasp the Spanish language! I can choose to be mortified and shrink back into myself. Or, I can burst into laughter too and enjoy a few bites of the delicious chops before heading on my way. I choose the latter.

Back in the sunshine, I am unclear of directions, so I decide to follow some pilgrims up a steep road that leads into the next town. About halfway up the hill, it occurs to me that I may not be heading in the right direction. I gesture to a woman gardening in her yard and show her my itinerary with the name of the town that is my destination. She points back down the hill from which I have come.

I point to another city along the way, and she points me in the opposite direction. I see that she is trying to tell me that up the hill is the shortcut. As I try to explain that I must go the other way to run into my friends, she shakes her head as if to say, *your choice— but it's a mistake.*

I thank her and take the alternate route back down the road into a tiny village. I see the small Church of Saint Irene and take it as a sign that I am on the right path.

I am rounding the last turn before leaving the village, full of lunch and uncertainty, when I hear my name shouted through a grove of trees surrounding a whimsical hotel garden. It is Jan and this is the hotel she is staying in tonight—mine is uphill through the woods to an unknown destination still miles away.

Never have I been so glad for company! Jan is sipping a goblet of red wine, sitting at a darling wrought-iron table in a lovely garden. She is visiting with other pilgrims who have just arrived from Nepal. I am thrilled to see her. It's been such a long day already and I am craving interaction.

Jan offers me a glass of wine and I hesitate. I must keep moving through the woods, up that steep incline again, and then who knows how long it will take to reach my hotel.

The wine goblet glistens in the sun. I am so relaxed now, boots off, toes wiggling in the grass. I suddenly understand the quandary of the recovering alcoholic with ten years of sobriety. I hesitate just long enough to consider … what will I remember at the end of my life? More miles of drudgery and solitude? Or some lovely wine in the late afternoon sun—enjoying the company of my friend and new pilgrims I have not yet met?

The decision is simple and complete. The first sip of wine flows right to my heart and soul, and a taxi takes me to my destinations as the sun sets.

Day 9—A Piece of Cake

Amenal to Santiago de Compostela—Nine Miles

It's a grand day. We all feel the buzz. It is just a short nine miles to Santiago, and we are ecstatic! No more foot care, or concern about clothing not drying. We are tossing out non-essentials left and right: Vaseline, wet wipes, duct tape, bandages. Freedom is in the air.

The six of us now walk together as fellow pilgrims and good friends. The necessity to walk quickly to our next destination has gone out of our step. We are exuberant, silly, carefree, and awed by the experience we have had. No more need to rush. We move at a leisurely pace throughout the day, sharing great memories, rehashing our journey, and laughing about all the crazy things we've experienced.

A musician is performing under a viaduct and my friends stop to dance joyfully as other pilgrims pass by.

We continue walking through small villages and woods until we notice that we are approaching a bigger town with bustling traffic. We glimpse Santiago in the distance and the first view of the far-off cathedral is thrilling. We know that we must first walk through the crowded center of town before we arrive at our ultimate destination.

We want to savor our Santiago experience, so after following the path through the city we make a group decision to stop for a beer or two before approaching the cathedral. It is the right call. We sit in a park just off the main street relaxing in the shade, sharing cool drinks, and tales of our journey.

When we see other bedraggled pilgrims trudging by, we leap to a standing ovation, shouting out and cheering them on to their final destination. They give us a thumbs up and we see that we have lifted their spirits ever so slightly.

Later we make our final ascent to the cathedral and it is magnificent! A man in full Scottish attire is playing a bagpipe inside the tunnel that opens to the cathedral courtyard. There are shouts, cheers, congratulations, high fives. A fervor fills the air as pilgrims acknowledge their accomplishment, celebrating with the friends they have made along the way.

We take photo after photo—each of us alone, now in groups, and always assuming the stance of pilgrim in full regalia. I stand proudly on the courtyard in front of the cathedral for my trophy photo. It is a day like no other—full of wonder and incredible joy. A life event!

That evening we dine on grilled octopus, sipping champagne and savoring the journey we have completed. We are one hundred percent satisfied.

Day 10—The Pilgrim Mass

Santiago de Compostela Cathedral

The six of us decide to stay in Santiago for the Pilgrim Mass at the Santiago de Compostela Cathedral and explore the town. We have set aside our plan to take a cab to Fisterra, sixty miles further along the path at the ocean, to see the true end of the trail. We are too exhausted and want a day of relaxation.

The centuries-old Pilgrim Mass is held daily at noon and it will be difficult to follow along since it will be spoken in Spanish, but it is an essential part of our journey. I arrive early and stand in a long line only to discover that the entrance is in another part of the cathedral. This is a huge cathedral with many doorways, large crowds, and time is running out, so it will be impossible to meet up with friends.

By the time I am inside the cathedral, the service has started, and all the benches are full. I stand with several others alongside a row of pews in one of the numerous wings of the cathedral. I am savoring this overwhelming experience. Powerful organ music fills the cavernous space, though it is impossible for me to follow the service spoken in Spanish.

When communion starts, some of the crowd begins to disperse. The thought has crossed my mind that I could easily slip out now too, but suddenly a group of young men in red velvet attire enter the altar area. I know instantly what this means, and a shiver runs through me.

The excitement heightens in the cathedral as it dawns on all of us that we will witness the swinging of the ancient *Botafumeiro*—the 120-pound brass fixture that swings, via a system of ropes and pulleys, through the cathedral dispersing incense to help clear the air (a tradition leftover from the time the first smelly pilgrims filled the cathedral centuries ago).

The *Botafumeiro* is only used after special masses and on other important occasions. The young men in red velvet will swing it across the cathedral at speeds of up to 42 mph.

I am in the perfect position to video the event and music accompanying it. Signs say that the use of cameras is forbidden in the cathedral, but no one is abiding by that rule.

With camera rolling, I begin to experience a most magnificent life event. It is beautiful, overwhelming, and fills me with awe. Tears of pure joy stream down my face and I feel the presence of the throngs of pilgrims who have come to this very place over thousands of years. It is the perfect end to a remarkable journey.

My Expectations

After a few more days winding down in Spain, I return home with profound gratitude about what I have just experienced. Though it was a magnificent journey, I also realize that my expectations and reality did not always align. What I expected to happen:

- Each morning I would enjoy leisurely breakfasts before starting the day's journey.
- It would be easy to get ready quickly each morning due to no makeup or hair routine.
- The trail would be mostly flat, winding roads in the beautiful countryside.
- Each day we would walk four to six hours, and then, after a quick nap, enjoy small-town nightlife.
- Every day I would have time for reflective journaling.
- Dinner conversations with fellow pilgrims would be engaging and frequent.
- I would keep up the pace of the pilgrims who started in Saint Piedmont.
- There would be plenty of time for shopping in cute little towns along the trail.
- I would be thinking deep spiritual thoughts throughout the journey.

My Reality

What actually happened.

- Exhaustion was a constant companion throughout the trip with a frequent need for breaks and water.
- Each morning took a minimum of one-hour prep time to get ready for the day's journey.
- The path consisted of one third of the time ascending, one third descending, and one third traversing flat land.
- Dehydration is real!

- Daily clothes washing takes time—some things never dry.
- After a strenuous day, interacting with fellow pilgrims can be exhausting.
- Most thoughts on the trail are not deep. Survival is first and foremost.
- To get over self-pity, I compared myself to civil war soldiers who walked barefoot in the snow.
- Would I do it again? Absolutely!

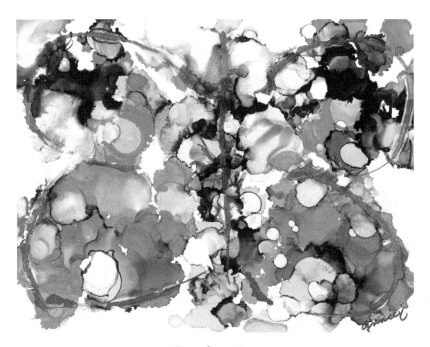

Transformation

Chapter 10

Messages, Insights, and New Direction

Reentry

Life seems so drab now that I am home from walking the Camino trail. The dreary days of November are a sharp contrast to the warm days of hiking through the hills and valleys of northern Spain.

It's odd to return to routine life without a self-imposed daily goal to surmount. I notice all the excess *stuff* in my life and wonder where it all came from—way too many clothes, an outrageous number of shoes—unnecessary clutter everywhere around me. The Camino has caused me to yearn to simplify and stay connected to the world that exists beyond the confines of my home and to-do list. The time outside has been magnificent.

I have heard that the Camino begins once you complete the journey. I believe it. I just can't get it out of my mind. While I was hiking, I was mesmerized by the beauty around me and can find nothing in my current life that comes close to replicating it.

It's been two months since I last met with Wes, and despite my great intentions to meditate during my journey, the only meditation I was able to engage in was when I silently trudged along the trail hour after hour. So much has happened in the past two months: contentious presidential elections, the Camino, a college reunion, best buddies in New Orleans vacation, and work that is piling up around me. I am exhausted.

One afternoon I grab my journal, curl up in the big green chair by the fireplace in my living room, and close my eyes.

COACH: So now what?

ME: I need to reengage in my inner life. I've had my numerology charted for the upcoming year. I am moving from a deep, spiritually evolving 7 Personal Year to an 8 Personal Year, which is all about manifesting.

COACH: What do you desire?

ME: More travel, collaboration, deep sharing and learning, vulnerability, strength, financial gains, philanthropy, music, dance, friendship, yoga, alertness, insight, wisdom.

COACH: You are hesitating. What is keeping you from also claiming channeling and psychic development?

ME: People have free will. What if what I see and share causes them to shift course and I am wrong or it does them harm, or I seem inauthentic or invasive?

COACH: Remember what Wes said: *Share only with permission.* You can just let others know that you are very intuitive. That's all.

ME: Okay—and then I will add psychic awareness. Lately, I've been thinking I should write a book with all these journal entries … maybe call it "My 7 Personal Year Journey."

COACH: Yes, you should! YAY! We've been waiting. We want that book to nudge others into their own spiritual journey. Remember how you let the pineal tones touch your heart and open you up? And how the journaling is taking you so deep?

We will help you write the book. Don't worry about the initial messiness. You already have a solid first draft. Speak from your book. Speak from your heart. Spark and inspire others.

I set my journal aside and I am lost in deep thought …

Birthday Brunch—Balloon and Champagne

It's mid-November and Sarah's first birthday without her mom. Several friends and family members are meeting up for a lavish birthday brunch at an upscale restaurant that would make her mom proud. It's good to be with Sarah. She has so many of her mom's great qualities: warmth, graciousness, and gratitude for this gathering. I know this is hard for her, but we are committed to having a great time, just as we would be if Irene were with us.

I've tied the long string attached to a birthday balloon to the back of Sarah's chair and it calls attention to the guest of honor throughout our brunch. The restaurant is crowded and festive. Tables are laden with delicious food and heavenly desserts.

After a leisurely brunch of delightful variety, we are working our way through assorted desserts when I suddenly notice a little boy, perhaps two- or three-years old standing behind Sarah. He has walked over from the other side of the restaurant and is pulling on the string of the balloon to look and perhaps play with it. Sarah notices the commotion behind her and turns around to smile at the little boy just as I see the boy's mother dashing to our table and profusely apologizing for the interruption from her son.

We are all amused and Sarah seems enchanted by the young child. She unties the balloon and offers it to him. He is thrilled. His mother is not. She insists that he should stop bothering Sarah. "We are *so* sorry. We'll leave you alone now."

But Sarah will have none of that and insists that we are almost done with brunch and he can have her balloon. Mother and son graciously accept the gift and return to their table—a happy child with a huge smile and a bobbing balloon.

Twenty minutes later, we are finishing dessert when our waiter appears with a bottle of champagne and glasses for all of us. He explains: "A family who just left the restaurant told us they wanted to send this bottle of champagne to your table to wish you a happy birthday."

Birthday Balloons

We are delighted! It is a grand ending to a lovely brunch. After toasting the guest of honor, we all agree that we suspect Irene sent that little boy over to the table and directed his parents to top off this birthday brunch with surprise champagne. Such a blessing!

Back to Meditation

A week later, I have my first session with Wes since returning from the Camino Trail. I tell him all about my travels and the synchronicities along the way. He listens attentively, asking me more about what I experienced, and shares his insights about what I may have been learning.

I tell him about the gift of walnuts from the old man in the countryside. Wes tells me that walnuts symbolize wisdom, knowledge, and inspiration. Native Americas believe the walnut symbolizes clarity and focus, gathering of energy, and beginning a new project.

When we meditate, it is deeply relaxing, and I realize how much I've missed going inward and quieting my mind.

Today we talk about accessing the heart through meditation. Wes explains: "You can focus on a small doorway leading into the heart. Picture a small bright light and make it smaller and smaller." This is how I can access deep energy within my heart, and I can direct it where it might help someone else. I envision entering the heart in a small rowboat to explore what lies within. It's a vast cavern that goes on forever.

Colors from the Spirit World

A few nights later, Irene visits me in a dream and as usual, I am thrilled to see her. In the dream, I was at the university library, writing a paper about some spiritual topic. After it was written, I was able to run it through a scanner that picked out the words in the document that held significant meaning.

In a way, this is what happens when I am journaling with Irene and with Coach. The words seem to flow and within the words, there is symbolism and meaning.

In the dream, she communicates to me: *Pale opaque blue is the color of the first level of spiritual understanding.* I recognize this as a reference to the blue necklace she was wearing in the first dream I had with her in March. It was the necklace that Sarah wanted to wear in the dream. Then she tells me, *the second layer of spiritual understanding is deep purple."*

I am intrigued. Why are the colors so important that she would share these insights in a dream?

Irene tells me that she knows I share her stories. She can communicate *through* me and she reassures me she is *right here all the time* and sometimes she misses being alive on earth. She urgently reminds me: *Ask me more questions!*

When I wake in the morning, I grab my journal and write.

ME: Okay, Irene, what do you want me to do with all this?

IRENE: Keep open. You'll figure it out. Talk to people about what I share—then they'll open up and more people will know.

I decide to lighten things up.

ME: How about the elections … can you believe it!

IRENE: So silly really—there's more important things to concentrate on. Helping people one by one so they can become ambassadors for the bigger realm. Ha! Listen to how I am talking about this! It seems so weird but it's so different here.

ME: How?

IRENE: There are no worries here. Kind of like having a glass of
           wine and thinking, *Whatever!*

           But there are also a lot of interventions to do. *Touched by
           an Angel* is not that far off.

           Those little acts of kindness come from heart and soul,
           and when we are doing things, it's like a big beautiful
           bonfire of love!

           The light in everyone flickers like a pilot light. We flick
           the switch on, and it bursts into flames. The flame—
           goodness, love—is the fiercest resistance to the pres-
           sures of the world around you.

           By the way, look for the symbology in the dreams. Look
           them up—I can keep it interesting.

A Visitation Dream

The following evening, Irene once again comes to visit me in my
dreams. In this dream, I am attending a leadership retreat and
there are many retreat attendees wandering on the beach outside
the oceanfront conference center.

Irene has come to join in the retreat. She spends some time out
in the sun and comes back tanned. I touch her arm just to assure
myself that she is really here, and though I am dreaming, her arm
feels warm to my touch.

I ask a guy in the group if he saw Irene and knows that she
died but is back with us? He smiles and says *yes*.

In the morning when I wake from the dream, I quickly grab
my journal and write.

ME: Irene, are you just coming to see me for old times' sake?
           Do you want to transition to the other side and be gone?

IRENE: I *am* on the other side. I like to visit you—you're my friend. You're open to seeing. I like how you get others to see.

I'll help you with your book—about what I'm telling you! I can get more specific.

First, I miss earth. We had fun.

I LOVE Sarah's new house and I know she is going to start feeling whole again soon. I will always live right in her heart.

My parents are here, and it's comforting, but in a different way. It's so reassuring to see them so happy together.

I will stay with you for a while to tell you what I can. I watch your meditations.

I can take many forms. Sometimes a stranger is smiling at you and I am living behind the smile. The old man with one tooth in Spain passed a blessing from me to you through his eyes.

We blend our souls with people on earth. Watch how I show up. Be sure to always look into the eyes of someone who has caught your attention. All of the loving souls are behind that.

Seeking Guidance from Coach

Later that evening, I journal once again with Coach, seeking some guidance for the story I am to tell in the book I am writing.

ME: Who will help me keep on a forward path, manifesting the book without getting burned out and thinking too much?

COACH: Calm Down! You'll be fine. Put one foot in front of the other—just like on the Camino.

Instead of getting up and walking, you will be getting up and writing until you have established a rhythm. It's easy when the words flow—Ha! It's your 7 Personal Year Journey to the Center of Your Soul!

Only it's not seven years—but the seventh year, which appears like slippery stones crossing the creek. Leap from one stone to the next. You do it alone and are also surrounded and supported. You can always call for guidance and then sometimes you must wait for the response.

ME: Today I saw a video of a dog rescue that had a huge impact on me. The dog had fallen into a fast-moving river and was perched on the edge of a deep waterfall, facing certain death if he were to slip over. On the side of the waterfall was a steeply slanting cement wall—rising 20 to 30 feet—and then a fence and a road.

A young man inched down the wall and into the water to rescue the dog. When he could not make it up the cement wall, three guys standing nearby had to form a human chain to try to pull the dog and man up.

The human chain was not long enough—they needed a fourth man.

Someone jogged by—glanced at the scene and kept going. Two other guys eventually showed up to help. Ultimately the two extra men were able to form a stronger chain with the first three to pull the dog and man to safety.

What does this mean?

COACH: You learn when you first try hard yourself—then call for help when you are at the end of your rope. This is how you learn.

If you ask or plead or beg too soon, where is the learning?

The guides and angels are always available, but not exactly at your beck and call.

You see we must discern just as you have to discern. We may want to help everyone, everything, but growth comes from others trying and grappling. And feeling frustrated. It's all part of the learning. Sometimes the falling apart leads to breakthroughs and triumphs! The men were thrilled to save the dog and we were all inspired. Do not help the butterfly escape the cocoon. All things in time.

Wisdom from Wes

The following morning, I tell Wes about the dreams and journaling from the past week. He reminds me that my numerology chart indicates that I have a lifetime challenge to be present in the moment! I know I have created so many structures around myself to keep me and my environment organized. Now I need to apply what I know to create new structure and disciplines (including carving time out to meditate, recharge, and stay in the moment).

Wes tells me, "It's time to walk away from 'I am doing this because this is what I've always done.'" He reminds me: "Think about what you've learned this year about self-awareness and self-care that you will want to apply to the business of the coming year."

According to numerology, I will begin my 8 Personal Year in January and this coming year will be all about manifesting, writing, and publishing.

Healing Breath

YEAR TWO

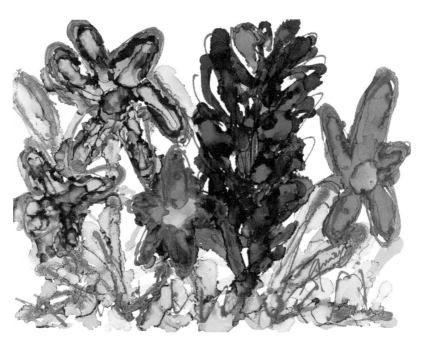

Raising High

Chapter 11

Guidance from Another Realm—Winter

December

It's been nearly a year since Irene's passing and I feel so blessed to be experiencing her presence through dreams, and journaling, and the many signs she sends to let me know she is around. I've reached out to a reputable, evidence-based medium, Missy Reno Smith, to see if she can connect with Irene and pass along messages from Irene to me. I want to know if Irene supports me in writing a book about our connection. It's a big undertaking and I want to honor her for the beautiful dreams and insights that she has provided throughout the year.

Missy is an acclaimed psychic medium from the Midwest. She was born with strong psychic gifts. She can see, hear, and feel spirits and angels from across the veil and as an evidence-based medium, she is able to convey incredibly detailed and accurate information about her clients' loved ones who have passed.

Years ago, Anne and I attended an afternoon class Missy taught about meeting our spirit guides. I was so impressed by her insights and engaging style that Anne gifted me a session with Missy for my birthday. A few weeks later, I scheduled a phone session with her to see if I could connect with some of my relatives who had passed.

Within a few minutes of starting our session, my father, grandparents, sister-in-law, and others came forward to communicate with me. Missy was able to describe each of them by personality, mannerisms, occupation, and even by name. It was remarkable. And all delivered with great warmth and care.

When a recording of the session arrived a few days later, I was able to listen once again to the specific and meaningful messages she brought to me through my loved ones. Such a precious gift.

For the past several weeks, since returning from the Camino trail, I have been thinking about reconnecting with Missy. I would be so grateful if Irene would come through during the session. Missy has never met Irene and knows nothing about her. I am wondering if she will be able to make the connection.

I recall that when I was meditating last evening, my head was tingling all around and into the nape of my neck, intensifying the experience. In the meditation, Irene was there, as well as Dad, and Grandma and Grandpa. Though they have all passed, they were in spirit showing themselves as human bodies to me. I felt them crowding me as though they were impatient to communicate with me.

I silently asked them, *Is everyone anticipating sharing messages with me tomorrow through Missy?*

They boomed a resounding *YES!*

Connecting with Irene

The next morning, I connect into our conference call and after a few minutes of conversation to get reacquainted, Missy begins. "There is someone here … a woman … and she's been waiting patiently to begin. She has thick hair … beautiful hair … BIG hair … sometimes bigger than at other times in her life."

This is Irene! Her thick beautiful hair has always been her crowning glory!

"She is holding her chest … her lungs and she says she went quickly, but it was not pneumonia. She's thankful and says that her breathing is wonderful now … and that her passing didn't make sense to her and that she was shocked. She says, '*Our minds were blown.*' She was not a smoker."

Missy explains that each of us comes to earth with a plan including how and when we are going to leave this earth. In Irene's contract, this is how and when she was going to pass.

Missy says, "We're always in God's timing—it had to happen then. Irene is turning the hands of a clock to show me."

Now she wants to talk about her daughter. She is giving love to her daughter Sarah—'*a mini-me.*' She is so proud of her beautiful Sarah, an amazing young woman who likes to give back and do good in the world. Irene talks to her daughter's little dog—communicates to her daughter through her little dog. Sarah should notice when her dog is reacting and say, 'Hi, Mom!' All animals are mediums."

(Later Sarah confirms that her little dog does act strangely at times, staring at her intensely or leaping up onto the bed to sleep on her chest).

"Irene says that Sarah is supposed to get into fundraising for children and she sees her at the top of the organization. She deserves the spotlight now. She does good and this will make her feel so much better. Irene is so proud of Sarah and has so much love for her entire family. Irene is sending love to her siblings and talks about her dad: 'everyone knows and loves him.'

Missy adds, "Everyone loved Irene! She has a very large circle of friends and acquaintances, and was honored and humbled to hear what people said after her passing."

Missy pauses and then says, "Irene was just with you taking a long walk."

I gasp! Then tell Missy about my long walk on the Camino trail.

Missy follows up: "Irene says, 'This was our journey together and I was with you EVERY SINGLE STEP OF THE WAY.' "

She adds "Every step you took, she took! She saw you sitting alone at the coffee shops along the trail and she sat with you".

I am laughing as I tell Missy, "I know that Irene would *never* be interested in going on such a journey in her earthly life!"

Missy continues, "She wants to acknowledge your growth and knows that you received a download from God and that it was a big one. She says you have reached a milestone—raised your vibration. It is like graduating—you have gained more knowledge and wisdom."

Missy notes that I might notice a change in the people around me and how I interact with others. The download has opened my awareness further, allowing me to become a better conduit to the spirit world. I ask Missy to clarify this.

She says, "Sometimes this means you have been infused with knowledge and awareness and are lifted. You are closer to God today than when you went on the pilgrimage and this is a wonderful, beautiful thing. This was a really big shift in you and Irene wants this to stand out today. You may notice more people are coming to you—they want to hear what you have to say. Like 'going grey': you've earned more wisdom and grey hairs. This download happened six weeks ago."

I quickly recall six weeks ago was October 20, the day I attended the Pilgrim's Mass at Santiago de Compostela Cathedral and witnessed the magnificent *Botafumeiro* soaring above the congregation. A truly remarkable event.

"Now Irene is talking about your daughter Jessica whom she sees as another daughter. You should tell Jessica that she has another guardian angel. Irene says you can say things to Sarah that Irene can't, so now she is returning the favor and watching over Jessica. Jessica and Sarah are sisters in spirit, and she would love to see them get together more.

"Irene says Happy Birthday to you! She knows it happened before you left."

(My birthday is in September—one month before leaving for the Camino Trail.)

"Irene mentions that her birthday is in the spring and you should make sure to eat cake! Maybe even a birthday pie—just because it's Tuesday!"

(Later I consult a calendar and find that Irene's birthday will be on a Tuesday this coming year.)

I quickly tell Missy about the birthday brunch we held for Sarah when she gave her birthday balloon to the little boy and then his parents gifted a bottle of champagne for the table.

Missy tells me, "Irene says, *I wouldn't miss these moments for the world!*

"Irene has found a good way to get to you—in dreams. She's becoming a guide for you—just one of your guides. She says you need to fight the thoughts where you wonder *Am I crazy?* Keep writing down what's coming through. That's important when it comes through in dreams. You might be getting a lot that you're not retaining."

Now Irene is laughing about having to give up her earthly views (of politics, for instance) and says now she understands that everything is perfect—there is no right or wrong. Whatever is meant to be, happens! The world didn't end. Everything is okay. We might not see that it is as it should be—as God planned.

"Missy," I say, "will you tell Irene I am thinking about writing a book and ask her if it is okay to share our story?" (I *still* need validation—even though Irene and Coach have already expressed their support).

Missy tells me, "Everything that comes through you belongs to you. We're all receivers—but most people are not aware of when they are receiving. Irene says you're to put your mark on it. They— your guides—can give it to you word by word or by concept—it ultimately comes from God.

"Irene is nodding *Yes* to the book, saying, *Go for it!* She's happy for you to do it. Irene says you have permission to speak for her—say everything you know she would say. She hopes you benefit in all ways from putting it out there—she'll be so happy to see it!"

Missy adds, "There is a story to tell—both a story and self-help. It's about healing and a journey. Has an easy-to-read feel, like a novel or a story. It makes people laugh and cry. It also tells well on screen. People are inspired by that type of read, so be open to it becoming a screenplay."

I smile as I ask, "Is this how Irene and I will get to the Academy Awards?" This has been our secret lifetime dream forever! Missy says, "Irene will continue helping you. Contributing. Now, she wants to make a big pitch to get this moving into novel format. She'll be journaling more entries with you. Irene says you should say EVERYTHING. Don't hold back. Say it all! Say everything you ever wanted to say and everything you think she would say. She says it's going to be your 'passion project.' It's going to be all-consuming. Share anything you want with Sarah."

Missy says it's always just a request—I only need to do what I am comfortable with.

Missy adds some advice for me: "Ask God for an amazing close to the story … an awakening, some sort of epiphany, how you've been healed. It's a journey plus photos. This story belongs in print. When you're in such a good place in life—like you are and Irene is—synchronicity shows up everywhere and there are beautiful signs. The book is so helpful for people. It's been given to you as a gift to others."

And with that our session ends.

I am blown away.

Not only did Irene appear for the entire session, but her comments referencing the Camino Trail leave no doubt in my mind that she was with me. I knew I felt her presence around me and now I have validation.

Irene is right—the book *will* be my *passion project*—it already is. I have five journals filled with entries of her presence in dreams and meditations, and her wisdom and insights need to be shared. I am merely the transmitter of her messages.

My passion project

Irene Weighs In on Missy's Reading

The next evening is December 2, and it is just three weeks until Christmas. I am physically and mentally exhausted from hours of Christmas shopping at the Mall of America, a four-story indoor mall so large the shops surround an amusement park. I've trudged for miles in uncomfortable shoes in a sea of shoppers, dragging too many bags. I want nothing more than to go straight home, crawl into my warm bed, and fall fast asleep.

By 10:00 p.m., I am home and in pajamas ready to sleep as long as it takes to rejuvenate. No sooner have I burrowed into my bed and taken that last deep stretch and sigh, when I become aware, through the tingling on my head, that I am being coaxed to get out of my heavenly bed and journal with Irene. I am Ebenezer Scrooge—cap yanked down and quilt to chin. I do not want to leave this warm cocoon.

I attempt a mental bargain. *Irene, If you let me sleep, I'll write first thing in the morning.* But she will have none of it and after fifteen minutes of fending off her insistence, I give in and grab my journal.

Snuggled beneath a thick blanket on my cushy green chair, I open the journal to a fresh page and write at the top: *Irene, what do you want to tell me?* I close my eyes, start guiding the pen across the page, and this is what I write.

IRENE: Reese, this is amazing and I'm so glad we had our session with Missy! I've been waiting for you to really get it. I know you do but I'd need proof too. I never could figure out how you came up with this stuff—now I know. (This was a reference to thoughts I used to share with her about life after death.)

It's different here but in a good way. I see everything at once and can move really fast—be in lots of places at once. I study here—I've got some "unlearning" to do from living on earth.

Debbie (her best friend who died five years earlier) and my father greeted me when I arrived. We hang out sometimes, but I am not with them all the time because their love is encoded on me one hundred percent of the time. I just *know* that our love and connection is forever.

ME: What does it look like there?

IRENE: Beautiful—light, sparkly. We see earth and loved ones, but this is a bigger and much deeper place. People here have seen the light—they don't have baggage, attitude, depression, a feeling of smallness. How could you? It's beyond anything you could imagine. There is so much to explore but I feel no rush—no judgment. I'm in my own pattern.

ME: But do you sleep? Eat?

IRENE: Yes, we want nutrition and to rest our souls, but we are also available 24-7.

ME: Do you have friends?

IRENE: Of course! Everyone is so open to connecting instantaneously!

ME: What do you do all day?

IRENE: I am everywhere. I still love the Hollywood stuff. I keep up with the drama, but it really is silliness—just a distraction.

People want to have fun and aspire to a more glamorous life—but really, it's just a part they're playing.
I drop in on William and Kate. Ha! (A reference to Prince William and Kate Middleton.)

ME: Are you going to leave us for good at some point? I don't want you to go far. Will you be with us?

IRENE: Always! Who knows—I may be back around. It's an option but I kind of want to reunite with my loved ones before I go back.

You can do this book, Reese. If I don't have answers, I will find them for us. I'd like to be a co-author.

ME: Tell me about our walk on the Camino trail.

IRENE: Well—there were plenty of ridiculous parts—like your photo with the guy with the leather shorts—I was cracking up!

(This was a reference to a photo that was taken outside a coffee shop where I stood, soaking wet in my poncho and hat, next to a hippy-looking guy wearing extremely short leather shorts and a cowboy hat.)

IRENE: I like Jan and Lory and the guys—great companions.

Santiago was amazing. Loved the mass. You and I were standing for the photo in front of the cathedral. Did you know I was there?

ME: I felt a little funny standing there all alone. Lory and Jan walked 500 miles—me only 125—so I had to tone it down.

IRENE: That's ridiculous! Grab the crown and quit belittling yourself. We're going to need to work with you before the book tour (which I will be on!). God wants you to speak truth, and *tell the story*. He (we) just proved it! We don't die and things are way better—easier and more loving—on this side.

Practice saying, "Through my friend Irene, I was sent a story that needs to be shared with the world, to bring hope and possibility, and to help us know we are never alone."

You know this to be true—it won't be hard at all. Pick good pictures—show them the light in my condo—and our silliness in London needs to be in there too.

ME: Thank you, dear friend. I am so grateful you are here. Let's go to Hollywood!

Irene, have I just read too much so my brain thinks I know all about the afterlife? Or, am I just remembering what is real?

IRENE: No, you are just remembering when you were here. Keep meditating—it will keep you grounded so you can work. Maybe I'll gather a group and we'll all give you stuff to write—we can critique and put things in an easy way to describe later.

How about some metaphors? Heaven is a twinkling snow globe—just delightful. I can listen to beautiful music all the time. I am never afraid to be alone as I travel about.

There were a few of us with you on the trail by the way. How about those ravines!

Thank you for missing me so much on day five.

Drinks with Sarah

It's Saturday afternoon and I have asked Sarah if we can meet for a quick drink and some snacks at Tavern. I can't wait to tell her I am writing this amazing story about her mother. How will she respond?

When we are settled in with a glass of wine, I tell her all about the session with Missy and read from my journal the messages from her mother as well as Irene's encouragement to write the book. I promise to send the recording of the session so she can hear all of it. Then I ask her how she feels about me writing the book. I will not do it if she doesn't want me to.

Sarah tells me that she is okay with me writing the story since it is what I have experienced. I feel a great sense of relief and I assure her that she will see the final draft before it is published.

Later that evening I open my journal and write.

COACH: Feel the fear and do it anyway! We wouldn't think of deserting you. We want these messages out in the world.

It will be a teaching for you to open people in organizations to the possibility of designing the life they were meant to live.

You've met your team before (spiritual guides), but now you know there really is a team. Good big strong football guys blocking and tackling anyone who gets in your way while you write. You heard the masters. They have told you that the messages will turn to gold—flow deep inside you and ground you—and then turn outward to pure gold for others. Do not be afraid. The fount is so vast—you could never say it all. We'll help you with content.

ME: Okay, Irene, what do you make of this?

IRENE: Pure joy—big guns helping. We're going on the road. Tell them everything.

I immediately recall a guided meditation I participated in years ago in a graduate class called "Psychological Transformation and the Spiritual Journey." In my meditation, I am standing in the center of a group of students who have formed a circle around me and they are sitting cross-legged on the floor. I have a wand and I slowly turn around the circle pointing the light-filled wand at each student to ignite their inner light.

It's an incredible feeling to expand the light by connecting with others.

I am building my power of light through connection—through igniting my students and through the light I receive downloaded through angels and guides from the spirit world.

Three Visits from Irene

On a Saturday morning mid-December, I am in my bathroom searching for Christmas wrapping paper on the bottom shelf of the linen closet. Suddenly, out of the corner of my eye, the electric weigh scale next to me lights up. I am two feet away from the scale, so I have not bumped into it, but the display light suddenly goes on for a long second or two, then goes off.

Several times throughout the day I return to the bathroom to bump the scale, gently nudging it into the wall—but the light does not come on. I find that odd but chalk it up to just a malfunction. It never happens again.

I crawl into bed about 11:30 that evening, peruse through Facebook, play a few rounds of "Words with Friends." Too tired to stay awake any longer, I fall asleep around midnight.

When I wake up in the morning, I quickly check my phone on the end table, as I do every morning, to see if my daughter has left me a text message in the night. I am shocked to see a text message from Irene sent at 1:06 a.m.! Instantly I have a sinking feeling in my stomach. This cannot be happening! Do I even want this to be happening?

I am momentarily paralyzed with indecision. What should I do? Irene has sent me a multimedia message but that can't possibly be true, can it? I leave the phone on the nightstand and head toward the kitchen to brew a big pot of coffee. I am pacing … a year's worth of messages culminating in a text message on my phone!

After downing my first cup of morning coffee, I finally click open the text message and see that it is blank, there is no image or message. I am flooded with relief. Though it would have been wonderful to get a message, it is also a startling idea. Now I know that Irene, and likely others in the spirit world, can communicate through technology and I wonder what is to come.

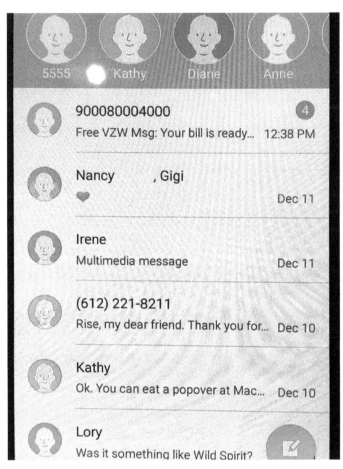

Irene's text message

On Monday I arrive at my session with Wes, bolt down the stairs to his studio, and can hardly wait to get his input about the text message and the scale lighting up. Thank God, he is nonjudgmental and does not question my sanity. He shares with me that for those in the spirit world, it is relatively easy to manipulate electronics and they find it to be a great avenue to communicate. He has heard similar stories from other clients he works with.

I find it alarming! If those events can happen, what else is possible?

That afternoon, Anne and I are at a company site consulting with employees. I am in one small conference room with a few clients; Anne is in another.

The conference room I am using has a large table, a projector, and the screen is pulled down to use for presentations. I spend an hour working with my small group, and then they are packing up their things to vacate the room. While I am putting away my computer, an employee sitting across the table picks up a remote control and raises the screen, then sets the remote back on the table and leaves.

When all the employees have left the room, the screen suddenly *on its own!* lowers back down again.

I am either getting to see the spirit world on a very personal level or I am losing my mind!

Anne's Turn for a Reading with Missy

I share everything I've been experiencing with Anne, and she is shocked to hear about the three visits from Irene.

She is as surprised as I am about my reading with Missy in which Irene spent the session communicating messages to me about the book.

Anne misses Irene as I do but has not experienced dreams and channeled messages from her, so our spiritual connection is a bit of a mystery to her.

Anne has decided that she will also contact Missy. She wants to see if Missy will be able to connect with her favorite Aunt Carol who passed a few years ago. Anne tells me she is excited for the session and will call me afterward to debrief what happened in the call.

A few days later, as Missy starts her session with Anne, she immediately tells her, "There is someone here. I met this same person during someone else's reading a few weeks ago. This is so unusual!"

Anne and I both know this is a reference to Irene coming through in Missy's session with me.

"Her passing started as symptoms and ended as something big. She has dark, wavy hair. She wants to call you sister. Wants to give you that love. Wants to pass on love and life for you.

"You guys (a reference to me and Anne) have so much going on. Everything is growing and changing."

Anne asks, "What is the change?"

"Personal life changes are coming up," Missy replies, "but not related to work. Could be a move. Some person or place is bringing you energy—it's big!

"You're changing your flow—putting on a different energy. Hmm ... is this a relationship change? No, it feels so BIG! This is a personal change. I don't see it in terms of negatives—it feels like a good change.

"Now, Irene is talking about painting in peacock colors—BIG, COLORFUL, BEAUTIFUL."

Missy asks Anne, "Are you going to take your pictures out to the public? Irene is seeing you bring the art out the door. A gallery. Lovely soothing watercolors.

"Irene is talking about 'going digital'—don't stop painting. Look at digital—it being mobile—bring it with you wherever you go.

"A gallery in California. Your work goes somewhere in CA. Irene sees WIRES—something 'see-through' as well. Maybe mount paintings on open glass walls.

"Irene says, 'Think big'! Paintings now are small, and card sized."

Missy is referring to the tiny framed watercolor paintings Anne gifted to Irene.

"Do some Big Stuff—try on a bigger scale. Painting on large sheets of plastic using ink and your breath.

"Flowers—orange and pink—like lotus—soothing—will draw a lot of attention.

"Put sparkly stuff in there too—shimmery powder. Iridescence.

"Create metallic and INKING with the watercolor. They go together. Bless the paintings."

Missy continues, "Irene is very focused on your art. The change may be about artwork or real estate … a space to show your work. Be open to the change, but don't go looking for it. When you look back you will recognize a REAL change. Open even more.

"Irene says you are so tuned in to the other side. Don't be surprised if some downloads are happening too. Stuff is going on at different levels in the spirit world.

"LOVITUDE—it's an awareness. Spread it for others to see, recognize, experience."

A Note About Lovitude

Lovitude is a word and a symbol that stands for Love and Gratitude, the two highest vibrations in the universe. Anne was inspired to coin the word Lovitude in 2005 when she was completing her thesis for her master's degree in Human Development and Holistic Health and Wellness. As she describes it, she was in the desert, working on her thesis when the symbol appeared to her. She had been creating images on a Buddha Board with a paintbrush dipped in water. Typically, the image would disappear after just a few seconds. When she painted the Lovitude symbol, it did not disappear, and she knew that the symbol was significant.

A few weeks later, she asked her friend Janel Russell, designer of the Mother and Child© pendant, to create a pendant and molds for Lovitude jewelry. Over time, Anne shared the symbol on a limited number of necklaces, charms, and a few other products, but for the most part, she had not referenced Lovitude much in the previous few years.

Lovitude Symbol

The Reading Continues …

Missy continues, "When you spread that energy (of Lovitude), you are injecting it and it spreads.

"Symbols—Logo—sell it. Irene wants to see it on everything. It's your 'Chosen Energetic Signature.' We choose our thoughts; therefore, we choose our emotions. Lovitude is the foundation.

"Irene wants to call attention to the fact that 'we choose.' Let others know that they choose too. She says, 'Keep wearing those SCARVES! It's gonna become a thing. You (meaning Anne and I) are going to give scarves in memory of Irene."

Anne asks, "Did Irene send Risë a text message?"

"Yes, she sent it," replies Missy. "*I just have to manipulate the technology*, Irene says. She's a pusher—her message to Reese was *Love you; stay on task!* She's active; she's there."

"Did Irene meet Aunt Carol?" asks Anne.

"Yes. Irene has animal magnetism—Aunt Carol has the same. They are getting along. Very similar. Irene is so happy to be in your world—watching over you from the other side. She's sending her love. She wants to make you some sweets. She's laughing—wants to put something sweet in your mouth.

"Irene says, *SNOWFLAKES are part of art*. She's seeing patterns. Not the real snowflakes. She's trying to weave the snowflakes in. They are overflowing beyond counting."

Now Missy says, "Someone famous is coming through! Snoopy is here and I keep hearing 'Sparky! Sparky!'

Anne tells Missy that Sparky is the nickname of Charles M. Schulz, creator of Charlie Brown and Snoopy. Anne worked for Charles Schulz and his team when she opened Knott's Camp Snoopy in the Mall of America. Anne was the marketing manager and the first employee hired before the grand opening.

Missy says, "Well, Charles Schulz says he's one of your guides, supporting you, and you'll have more stamps than he did. His message is *Trust what you're getting! What you're receiving. Trust! You have permission to speak for the other side—use it—take that.*

"You're a breath of fresh air—speaking the truth. You have lots of confidence. You're doing everything right."

What Do We Do with All This?

No sooner is Anne's reading with Missy finished than we are on the phone debriefing everything. I am as astonished as Anne is that Irene came to both our sessions.

The reading with Missy has left Anne with more questions than answers. "What am I supposed to do now?" she asks me. "I'm not an artist and I don't know anything about painting on plastic, blowing ink across the page. How am I supposed to act on that?"

I can see clearly that Anne is not ready to do anything with the message she has received until she figures out what it all means.

As the Christmas holiday draws near, both of us are overwhelmed with the busyness of the season and with our clients. We will put on hold our directions to write a book and to create large paintings until after the holidays when we are relaxing at the Omega Institute in Costa Rica.

Ongoing Transformation

Chapter 12

Expanding Awareness

Yoga Retreat

It is the first weekend of the new year, a year since Irene's passing. Anne and I are at the Blue Spirit Retreat Center in Costa Rica for a week of *gentle* yoga (see chapter one). I still cannot believe that I am staying at this rustic resort in this beautiful paradise.

Each day, there are early morning and late afternoon yoga sessions, beach time, pool time, and hours to read books and explore the property. I have plenty of time to reflect and journal throughout the week. On the second night when most guests have gone to their rooms, I find a cozy seating area tucked away from the main lobby and open my journal to write.

ME: How is it that I am here?

COACH: We made sure you could come. There are things to see here and we wanted you to be open to new learnings. Irene is here too, and many others. You are learning about simplicity, acceptance, and not needing to know. Nature surrounds you so you can write. Listen carefully for messages.

IRENE: Hi Reese. Do not look to the sky to see me and others. We are all around you. Think of angels in the sky as just projection—like Disneyland's Haunted Mansion. We are all around you and in you. We also love to help you. Just call on us to bring love and support to those who need it.

Today we had you meet Lynn (a fellow yoga participant). It was important for you to hear her story about her adopted son who was diagnosed with severe mental illness, and how ultimately that stress pulled her marriage apart. She has learned that when brain waves are scrambled, we create new neuropathways through love.

Here is a challenging earthly test. Can we move past mind confusion and help all who cry out?

ME: But, Irene, how do we guard ourselves against anger and destruction? Lynn said her son projected violence, rage, manipulation, lies, fabrications, and threatened to kill himself and her.

IRENE: By calling on us and by sharing who you authentically are—pure love, no judgment, incredible love. We do not control others, we do not stop the destruction, but we have power to access God so that healing and miracles can occur.

ME: Is it crowded where you are?

IRENE: No, because we are energy. We collapse into each other and merge our souls collectively. We expand and contract effortlessly. We can't bump into each other and there is no feeling of flesh bumping into flesh. But I am more alive and real here than on earth. We are all amazingly fast and mobile.

ME: Tell me more about what you see and know.

IRENE: Well, it's like this resort you are at near the ocean (very good for you!). You are far from home, and you know it is the cold winter, and people are huddled in joy or steeped in isolation back home. There are some who are thinking of you and you can feel a twinge or fluttering in your heart knowing they are thinking of you.

If someone cries out, lost in the mountains, or if someone is crying out in pain or sorrow anywhere—no matter the *faith* they practice or do not practice—we are there to support them.

Sometimes a group of us sweeps in to help and it's always so much fun. Other times, I may go alone. I love the human spirit. We can manipulate circumstances, so people can get the help they need.

We comfort and can help by moving situations around. We don't meddle. Earthlings are babies learning to crawl, then walk, then run. We just bring love.

If you want to stare at flowers or into people's eyes or at the beautiful sunset, do so and remember that everything we focus on intensifies. Focus always on what you are moving towards—what you desire. Reese—what is that for you?

ME: Pure love, openness, courage. I want to be a warrior, teacher, sage, mentor, coach, companion, lover.

IRENE: Reese—I am always with you. I go to all the fun places with you. I'm loyal. I get guidance on how to be even more discerning in the help I give.

Now, Coach jumps in with some other important insights.

COACH: Irene is your *Pen Pal from the other side*. She willingly and ecstatically volunteered. You have much more to learn. You can levitate, completely change your energy from your body, fine-tune it like an instrument, use your mind to move energy at will. Why does no one see how easy it is? Practice—really. It's common.

We need you on earth now—your work is so needed. Do not make assumptions about understanding everyone's spirituality—do not judge.

Remember that some say they are closest to God in nature. Everyone has their way.

Use your curiosity—we gave it to you. Drop judgment and you can do this work. See all as God—all as good. We will bring you to the right places like this. We will raise the vibration forever, so this is truly heaven on earth.

ME: Thank you! I am grateful to serve.

Blue Spirit Resort hideaway

Day Three—Costa Rica

It's the third day in paradise and I am at our afternoon gentle yoga class. Thank goodness this is not an advanced course. I'm a bit challenged with right and left, so sometimes I find myself in a modified yoga pose, accidentally facing one of the other yogis who is facing me in a contorted yoga position.

I compliment a woman on her ability to stand on her head in perfect form for a good minute or two. She graciously shares three helpful hints on head poses I could try with various levels of ease (a dialog cloud forms over my head … *God, No! Do you know how old I am?*)

I am most challenged with planks and sitting cross-legged, back straight. There is simply not enough bend in my upper body. Who knows how I would get there? I stretch gently—nothing—stretch a little harder and now I can do it but cannot breathe. Thank God, I am in the corner of the room.

I try the planks—do the best when I can—but I notice my palms are screaming for intervention and my knees are so much better on my foam pad (which I have tossed to the side).

Well, live and learn. It's my fourth day of yoga sessions—yay me. I am all about the gentle stretches until I really know those poses and can loosen up.

I've had a "body essence" massage this morning. Just glorious—from a kind German woman with soulful eyes and a supportive nature. I lie on the massage table, eyes closed, and without touching me, she runs her hands slightly above my body, as though she is scanning me. Now she is ready to begin and she tells me she is focused on the areas where the energy is blocked in my body. It's a relaxing half hour and when we finish, she gives feedback about what she energetically picked up about me.

She sees that I am extremely sensitive with a big heart and very tuned in to the environment. She knows that I can *hold space* and pull people together … and that I am solid and grounded.

She tells me to take care of my body. Ask it what it needs. Over time I will get more comfortable in my body and more emotion and laughter will be released. She tells me I have *stored laughter!* I definitely want to get that out!

She's right. I do not get nearly enough exercise and fresh air as I should. My body can feel cumbersome and slow me down. Then I am frustrated, and I feel badly about myself (see Day 5 Meltdown on the Camino trail).

I need to rise above my ego constraints and work on opening my heart even more. Let the laughter flow!

More Guidance from Irene

The next day, I've been thinking about the massage session, numerology, predictions about what is on the horizon in my life. I need to be aware of opportunities and take some of them that arrive. Take a chance—be daring.

I grab my journal to write with Irene.

IRENE: There's a script up here about your life. You can follow it to a tee, but you have free will. Do you want to know what's in store for you? Then think of the most positive and amazing life that you desire and that's what's in store for you. Every day is a million decisions—work or not work; be aware or unaware. If you are living your best life you stay in the moment and make decisions one at a time for what is right for you.

Another glass of wine? Or call it a night, staying alert and ready to face tomorrow.

You stand in who and what you are, and it's a big table of precious gems you are attracted to and are attracting. Some you can rule out and then you narrow your choices, but still, you must choose.

ME: So how do I choose?

IRENE: By following your heart and intuition. What is holding you back? Fear? That's nothing. You assume others do not feel fear, but they do. So be a role model for fearlessness.

ME: Irene, what can you share today?

IRENE: Your massage therapist was perfect for you. She reminds you to feed all your senses. Bring yourself as alive as possible every day. There are so many people in half-dead states walking around. You yourself have lived days at a time so wrapped up you have been unable to see the beautiful world. The Costa Rica people are beautiful, kind, gentle … able to make soulful connections no matter what personality they come in. You have seen this—now you can resurrect this beautiful way.

This IS a jungle book!

ME: What to remember about yoga:

- I am capable! No worries about how I look—everyone is on their own.
- Deep breathing is key! (Today, I worked up to eight counts on my exhale.)
- Keep working on one-leg balance.
- Block, pillows, knee pad, forehead cloth are all very helpful.
- Save your hands by shifting back on downward dog—have your hands closer.

What to remember about eating healthy and clean:

- Eat veggies at every meal.

- Add spices, occasionally nuts, jazz up rice.
- Tofu is okay. Plantain is okay too.
- Water is essential—all the time!
- A little meat goes a long way … or learn to like beans!

Moving to Higher Levels of Awareness

One evening a few weeks after I return from Costa Rica, I am led on a guided imagery meditation and experience an energetic cone surrounding me as I am guided to higher levels of awareness. I am being lifted to the level of the highest vibrations—though, of course, there is always so much more.

I start writing in my journal and Coach immediately leaps in, and then Irene.

COACH: There is incredible awareness here. This is the level of manifestation where anything is possible. All creation happens here, and it is beautiful. Earth is such a fascinating drama—though some experience painful lives.

Ponder this: how can you lead others to this place above and beyond? There is comfort and knowingness here.

ME: Irene, is this what it's like for you to live within such high-energy vibration? It feels amazing.

IRENE: Yes, we go far away and then we come in and hover around wherever help is needed.

I am going to the Women's March on Washington this weekend. We love the energy that is around now. People are waking up to the energy around them … in this case, there is resistance to the unrest in politics right now. We are engaged—on edge—ready to support at a moment's notice.

This is a natural state of being. We should live there always. Reese, I feel your support.

ME: What do you want me to know today?

IRENE: Practice dissolving into your energy and come out to play on these higher realms. You can see me and still be on earth.

If you dissolve into or infuse with higher energy, you will see more places where you are needed for help and we can infuse our love through you so you can do heavenly tasks.

ME: Irene, I'm practicing. Where is my help needed now?

IRENE: In the pages of the book. Tell them what they can access: pain points and solutions.

Ask your readers, *Do you want a simple manual? A user's guide? If yes, do this:*

- Relax and quiet your mind.
- Go inside to settle, then open to a higher vibration.
- As soon as you do, thoughts come into your head: *Who needs assistance? Who are my helpers?*
- Connect heavenly guidance and healing to those people whose souls are crying out. And places: Is there a decrepit building in need of repair? A simple smile to the one who is open to remembering where they have come from?

You must be aware in each moment. Send love and energy with no expectation … just a wink and a smile.

COACH: Yes, if you can come closer to us, you will experience much more expansiveness. It will be effortless. From here, you see the bigger patterns. Then you see that where the energy bunches up, that may as well be earthly drama. It goes away as quickly as you can direct energy for healing and cleaning the energy field.

Journey to higher realms

Mid-January Meditation—Journey to My Soul

I am settled in for an evening meditation. I click on the audio link to one of the guided imagery meditations on my computer, but the computer randomly clicks on another link. That's odd. Didn't I just listen to this meditation last night? I decide to go with it.

Sitting in my green chair, I close my eyes and begin to sink into the meditation, blocking out all distractions from the outer world. A few minutes later it feels as if I have left my body and I am now experiencing myself as my soul. I look down at my body and see that it has shattered, and I am experiencing my soul as a flowing dancer with fluid movements, radiating great joy. She loves bare feet, sheer clothing. She spins and dances with arms outstretched and is filled with beautiful light.

She needs balance and toned muscles—lean body—for those movements. She enjoys real food—juicy flavorful fruits and vegetables—but she does not lead a life of restriction or sluggishness. No shuffling along because she is exhausted.

The movement and the music bring her alive and fills her with the deepest joy. The music dances her—free-flowing and exquisite. Her soul on earth brings a light that emanates from her body, through her movements and her eyes.

Life is to be lived at a glorious pace … just right for her. She is an artist.

No harsh judgment or frantic fixing. She lives as one with all and has wisdom beyond her own knowing.

I have seen glimpses of her in imagery, in my future map, in the most relaxed places in my mind. Her industriousness is effortless. By movement alone she accomplishes. She glides, head high, with intention of such great clarity that it manifests itself.

Maybe she needs to be back in Costa Rica. She can breathe there and move without effort. She can be in the jungle with the monkeys howling, and somehow it feels like home. Like paradise.

I am in a dream—how do I sustain this amazing vision?

I look at my journal and see that my penmanship is beautiful, flowing, curved, gliding across page after page.

Back to the Temple of the Masters

The next evening, I again turn on my computer to experience a guided meditation. I breathe deeply, center myself, and then lift my awareness to a higher level. Once again, I am on a journey to the Temple of the Masters. When I arrive, it is the temple with the beautiful courtyard, but then I am guided to go higher, past that temple, to an even more expansive temple with exquisite, brightly colored walls that continuously pulsate as the colors change.

I am trying to resonate at this energy level so I can stay in this magnificent place and experience the pulsating colors.

Instantly, I am aware that I am now on stage in front of a crowd of thousands. I wear a flowing white robe and I am speaking to the crowd about our spiritual essence and our connection to the realms—how our soul comes down from the heavens to fill the cavity that is our body and we can expand our soul to the higher realms.

A master guide who has been with me in many lifetimes steps forward and I see that it is Wes—though not the Wes I know on earth. This is the ancestral, eternal soul of Wes who has lived many lives. Other guides are here too.

Later, after this meditation, I recall my first numerology session with Wes a year ago. When he looked directly at me and asked, "What are you feeling, right now, in this moment?"

I suddenly felt powerful energy surrounding him. I responded, "I feel as though I'm seeing you in human form in front of me, and I also sense that I am in the presence of masters."

After this exhilarating meditation, I journal with Coach.

COACH: Energy expands, contracts, reaches, all without effort. It congeals in sacred places we create, churches, peaceful marches for love (e.g. the Women's March).

Here we are all so busy, we need earthly helpers who are open to help. We need you and you need to attract others.

Be an observer and conduit for love. Say kind things, be kind. Never fear—we watch over you and know what we want you to do.

Get clear on your message. The pieces will fall together in the book. You've created the jigsaw puzzle—we'll supply the missing pieces.

Then you will walk to the stage and simply share. You are not trying to DO anything!

Be clear—set an intention—speak your intention.

Tell them, *This is a story of love and connections and a journey to the higher realms. It is an experience I want to share with you because it has come through me. I am only the conduit arranging the pieces to tell a compelling story.*

Notice where the words pierce your heart. There are warriors with loving messages they want you to hear.

Why? you ask. Because you can create peace for yourself and others. You can open to resonate at the vibration of love for yourself—and then a natural output of these higher vibrations will lift others.

What brings you to pure bliss? Walking in the woods? The innocence of small children, animals? The beauty of nature, creativity? Name it and claim it.

I pause now and I notice that my big ME—my Higher Self—is transmitting to me constantly in my dreams, through others, and through how I feel. It's preparation for *Stepping into the fire and standing still*. But the fire is not there to harm me. It is a bold energy that I can embrace. I can walk and emanate fire and divine energy. Have fun, be real, and walk in harmony and assurance that all is exactly as it should be.

ME: How do I capture on paper a journey beyond what I already think is the highest I can go?

COACH: How do you sustain this wave of warmth and energy?

ME: I don't know—it's BIG and my limitations of brain and physical body won't budge sometimes to allow all of that energy.

COACH: Ha! Human constructs. You just *think* you cannot have a full experience, but that is a limitation you put on yourself. You can feel it—so why not trust your sense of knowing?

Can you not imagine sitting outside the upstairs yoga room at the Blue Spirit Retreat Center and feeling that space all around you in all directions? You are a space holder and with intention, you can expand your energy and attract what you need.

You'll want that loving energy with you as you spread that energy throughout the chapel or hotel ballroom or amphitheater or onstage in front of the crowds.

You are open. We see that. Now it's time to do more expansive energy work. Practice manifesting, sending energy and light.

We promise that messages will come through your heart and hands, so you can write this powerful book. It is a door we have opened for you—and when finished another door will open up—a place of higher spirituality.

When you trust this energy, you will know exactly what you need to write. A language simple and sweet and non-threatening, bringing pure energy and joy.

Guidance from Coach—February

Now that I have Irene's support to write the book, I feel mild tension about what needs to be added to the content from my dreams and journal entries. I decide to consult with Coach for support and direction.

ME: What more should I include in the book?

COACH: It is only necessary to tell the story infused with your personality. When you write, we're writing through you. Get out of your own way. We see your intention is good and true. There is no need to embellish—it's so amazing as it is.

We think you are exactly the one to do this—but step away from any heaviness or feeling like you must *be legit*. Just be yourself—fun, a bit irreverent, wanting to bring others along on the journey.

We are going to hound you on this—get a plan in place. You will LOVE the results.

Irene is gifting you this knowledge and experience. She loves you and respects your communication style. Trust her. Ask her questions. If she doesn't have the answers, she'll get them.

ME: How do I know this is not my ego talking?

COACH: You don't. Ha! We work together. You're thinking and then intuition jumps in. You don't have to prove anything.

Nothing comes from striving and trying too hard—being too invested.

ME: What wisdom belongs in the book?

COACH: The stories of communication across time and space.

Manifesting

A few days later I experience a guided imagery meditation about manifesting what we desire. It is an exciting and amazing experience and I quickly open my journal to write with Irene.

ME: Irene, where are you?

IRENE: Right here. How cool that you created those beautiful pink flowers in meditation. See how easy it is to create? But it is meant to be for the good ... for love, peace, harmony.

Remember that you can also create from fear—that is the dark place. Focus on the flowers and what brings you joy! You should just see the flowers *here*!

I miss going to the breakroom with you for a cup of coffee, maybe some muffins, cookies, pie. We can have a coffee break here. I'll envision coffee and catch the energy of it—recreate the taste.

ME: Who guides you?

IRENE: Many levels of energy ... like water ripples ... layers and layers ... all good. All-powerful, magnetic.

You feel the pulsing here—there is just so much. It's like living in your body at a high vibration. It's a pulsing that feels magnificent. Like that feeling when you are taking a nap and just when you drift off—well, it's surrender—even though over here you don't *surrender* old ways—they fall away. At least they did for me.

Do you remember having measles or chickenpox? You're sick—spots all over you. And one day they're just gone, and you are well, and you are past it. Well, that's what it's like here. We're over the illness of earth. (Ha! That's so negative, sorry!) And because we're on the other side, we want to encourage those we serve on earth. Cheer them on their journey by being by their side. Earthbound people get glimpses of the divine, but then it slips away.

Keep writing—there's so much more. Come up here and we will experiment, so you can feel the pull of the energy ripples.

I'm so glad you're here. I love you, Reese.

ME: Namaste. Thank you, Irene.

Manifesting flowers

Chatting with Coach and Irene About Striving

It's mid-February and I am working on the book, but it is so easy to get distracted. I decide to journal with Coach and Irene to gain some insight.

COACH: How are you doing?

ME: I'm on a fast-moving path—that conveyer belt at the airport. People are walking alongside me—but they are going more slowly—oblivious that they could be carried along faster.

COACH: What's the rush? Stay in the moment—take in the scenery. Quit striving whenever possible. Trust that all things are revealed in time. Use your intuition, speak truth, come from love, be expansive, allow the flower to unfold. You don't always trust the messages—which is ridiculous! Why are you stopping?

ME: I want to trust one hundred percent in the messages I receive. My tricky ego needs to sit on the sidelines, but it likes to creep in during visualizations, meditations, journaling.

COACH: Embrace your ego with love.

ME: Irene, are you out there?

IRENE: Nope—right here. Don't make me into an angel or a ghost. It's just me. What's up?

ME: Oh, I don't know. Just wanted to say hi. I'm going on a road trip to a Blues Fest. Wanna go?

IRENE: Of course! Even if you hadn't asked, I'd be there. You know I love car trips.

ME: What's going on up there?

IRENE: I've been exploring. No matter where you go here, you are NEVER afraid—never far away—always within a thought of having others around.

I have been to some magnificent mountains. I sort of fly around them. I come upon an incredible site or place and I can merge into the experience of it. Many others may be there too—but they clear out if you want them to.

I find groups that vibrate at a level that attracts me and I merge with them. Really wonderful. There is no judgment—one group over another. So I move about—you know I love to explore.

We talk to each other—share stories about where we've been—what our earthly experience was like (if we lived on earth). Some of the beings have not been to a school like earth, but they can sense where humans get stuck energetically and try to assist.

Everyone thinks that we—over here—have this massively angelic presence. But that's nonsense. I'm just little old me. I can hang out with anyone I want and (you're not going to believe this) I can infuse a bit of my soul into others so in that moment I can share the soul of someone else.

Think about that! If I want to merge with anyone else I can! Housewives of Beverly Hills, Princess Kate, Ha!

I can infuse some of myself into you as you write so you can *see* when you are speaking the truth and when it's fluff!

A Gift of Heart

A few days later, in a guided imagery meditation, I am led to a huge crowd of loving people out in a field. I merge with them and feel that I am bringing myself to a higher vibrational level.

They give me a gift and, at first, I think it is a large red velvet heart pillow, but then I notice it changes into a large vibrating heart. The message is that I am to go back to earth and allow this heart to keep open and activated as I walk the earth, beaming love and non-judgment and openness.

I open my journal and write.

ME: Guidance, please. Who wants to speak?

COACH: We'll step in. Keep up the good work. The book is chugging down the tracks. The book is moving already. Keep the cars connected—each with precious cargo. Do NOT get derailed.

Computer troubles? We'll fix 'em today.

Your aunt is here. (My favorite aunt passed away a few weeks ago.) She's going through an initiation—like a cleansing, a spa, an opening to our world. She is not sad, because she knows she is also on earth but in the layers of energy that surround loved ones—even trying to bring love into some tough places.

ME: I am hearing ringing in my ears. Who has something to say?

COACH: A wave of change for the better is coming on earth. Innocence versus greed. The voices of young school children are being heard throughout the schools and the world and the universe.

Ask Anne to paint "Change is rising." There is great hope, rebirth, translucent new energies, opaqueness, no boundaries, no borders. On and on the good vibes flow and spread.

(A few months later Anne creates her first Lovitude soul paintings called *Sobbing Universe* and *Hope*.)

ME: Thank you, everyone. I will practice patience with myself today. Please guide me to those who will help.

COACH: We are the highest aspects of you. You think we are *other* and are out there somewhere—but we are within you, coaxing you to come be with us in the heart space that you are on earth to teach and love. We are your team supporting you. It took time to remember us "big brothers and sisters," and now it's getting close to the time when we will have you speak. There will be no fear—only joy and guidance and love.

We are your ancestors though we seem to be outside you. But no, we are all multidimensional. Irene is an aspect of you. An angel in disguise. A Soul Sister.

Suzanne Giesemann—Serving Spirit I Workshop—March

Suzanne Giesemann has come to Minneapolis and I am attending her workshop, Serving Spirit I; my first experience of mediumship training. Curiosity has led me here. I wonder, *Do I have the ability to connect with those who have died and communicate messages from them to their loved ones still on earth? Well, aren't I already doing that with Irene?*

I will have plenty of opportunity to find out. Practicing in pairs throughout the workshop will strengthen our abilities to tap into the energy surrounding others—whether to read them psychically or connect with their ancestors and friends who have passed.

If I can make these connections, I will feel more confident that I truly am communicating with Irene's spirit and not just making things up. And what about Coach? We communicate as old friends, yet I know he does not reside in this physical world. Will I now trust his insights and messages more?

Suzanne helps us to get centered and raise our energy levels to connect with the spirit world. She explains to us that a psychic can tune into the energy field that surrounds another person to communicate what is going on in their world. A medium connects with a higher vibration level of people who now live in the spirit world. In this training, she will teach us to raise our vibrational level to connect with the higher energy field where spirits reside.

We are told that we must trust our intuition and that since no medium is a hundred percent accurate, we have some leeway. I am so relieved to hear this.

Suzanne is an amazing teacher and patiently leads us step-by-step through processes that raise our energy vibration. We are taught to connect with our guides to assist in the process and are shown the importance of setting a clear intention to connect with spirit in a way that will bring the greatest good for the sitter. We also need to set an intention that we are protected in this work—that lower energies are not allowed to come through in the reading.

She reminds us throughout the weekend about how important it is to train our minds to be still through a daily practice of meditation and prayer. In this way, we intensify our ability to be present in the moment and trust in the messages we receive.

We learn practical ways to receive messages, including symbols and signs we can depend on that represent concepts in the physical world. For instance, in our mind, we may equate an older woman who appears to us with grey hair and wire-rimmed glasses as a grandmother. Or, we may see a hard hat and that is our indication that the person worked in construction.

Suzanne teaches us that there are many ways to sense the energy of those living in the afterlife. For some mediums, spiritual messages come as words clearly spoken in their head. For others, spirit might appear as a sensation in their body, a gut feeling that brings with it important messages. Others sense spirit as a form of indistinguishable light or an energy that comes to them.

When I tune into the energy around me, I sometimes see spirits in physical form resembling what they looked like on earth—though younger and healthier looking than when they passed. If I were an artist (and I am NOT), I could paint a portrait of them with facial features, clothing, and their distinct body language. When I see Irene, she looks healthy and youthful, filled with love, light, and energy.

We are taught to ask questions (in our minds) when spirit appears to us, to verify that we are receiving accurate information. I might silently ask, *How did you pass?* and see a symbol from the spirit that gives me that information. Once I silently asked a female spirit how she died, and she grabbed the side of her waist. Later I found out that she had quickly passed with internal injuries sustained from a car accident.

The most important guidance we receive is to remain "compassionately detached" in our work and to focus on gathering information that can later be verified by the sitter.

By the end of Saturday, we have many tools that will help us psychically read others and connect with spirits through mediumship.

A Chance Encounter

On Sunday, the second day of training, we have more opportunities to practice what we have learned by *reading* each other as psychics first and then as mediums. When I am the sitter, I am amazed how often Irene shows up for me. I always know it is her as they speak of her bubbly personality and love of the feminine things in life: luxury, jewelry, dancing. Then they speak of her quick passing with problems in her lungs and once again we are connected. One reader tells me that Irene has her hands on my shoulders and is congratulating me. I wonder if her congratulations are because I am going so deeply into this learning.

We have a brief exercise in which we are to psychically *read* a new partner. After a few minutes, Suzanne will tell us to shift into the role of medium, connecting with our partner's loved ones on the other side.

I am paired with a nice guy named Scott and as I focus on him, I quickly pick up on many aspects of his life. For instance, I see him walking in the woods, and sense that he is an avid nature lover with a deep knowledge of birds and other wildlife. Then my focus shifts and I see him with friends from many areas of his life, groups who do not know one another, groups who have quite different conversations.

I feel as though I am just making everything up—yet I also know that there is truth in what I am seeing.

Next, I see Scott on a stage and when I focus in on this image, I realize that he is not teaching or giving a presentation but is the Master of Ceremonies for a large event. This seems odd to me, but I am going with what I see.

After five minutes, Suzanne directs us to shift our focus to see from the perspective of a medium. I look back at Scott and instantly notice the appearance of an older gentleman behind Scott's left shoulder. I perceive him be a great uncle; he has a physical resemblance to Scott.

Quickly I pick up on another scene. In it, several males are lounging in a living room on overstuffed couches. They are enjoying each other's company immensely, joking and bantering with one another lightheartedly. I suspect that they are family members and they are a jovial bunch.

During feedback at the end of our practice session, Scott confirms that yes, he is a nature lover and has several groups of friends who do not interact with one another. He also tells me that he has been told he resembles an uncle who passed long before he was born. He suspects the group are other uncles who have passed.

Then he tells me that he is indeed an emcee at the International Association for Near-Death Studies (IANDS) annual conferences, and I intuitively know that this is a conference I *must* attend.

He gives me a quick overview of this amazing conference that hosts researchers and scholars from around the world who study higher consciousness. The conference includes many attendees who have had near-death experiences where they left their physical body and visited the spiritual world. These individuals may have died in a car accident or on the battlefield or on the operating table. And then they come back to life or out of a coma minutes or hours later. They come to the conference to share what they experienced and to be in the presence of others who have experienced something similar and can support them.

This August, the annual conference will be held in Colorado and will be attended by 400 to 500 others. I am beyond excited and am certain that I will be attending this conference, as will Anne. It is non-negotiable. This is a sign for both of us that it is the next step in this journey Irene has put us on.

Blowing Through

Chapter 13

New Life Opportunity—Spring

The Birth of Lovitude Soul Painting

It's been two months since Anne, Patrick, and I were at the Blue Spirit Resort in Costa Rica, and I notice that Anne has been much more withdrawn since we returned home. When we meet up from time to time, she tells me that though she is focused on her client work, she cannot figure out why she is not motivated to do much else. Her December session with Missy has left her wondering what she is supposed to do with the specific directions to bring Lovitude to the world in a big way, starting with painting on large sheets of plastic using ink and her breath. She reiterates, "I'm not an artist!" so the directions from Irene seem abstract and impossible.

One day in early March, Anne and I meet to discuss our client work and catch up with each other's personal lives. Suddenly she grabs her cellphone and says, "I have to show you this. Look, on March 30 it says in my cellphone calendar 'New Life Opportunity' at 7:00 a.m. I have no idea what that even is. Did I sign up for a conference ... do you remember? I guess I'll just erase it. Really, I did not put that there."

Early the next morning, Anne calls and excitedly tells me, "I erased New Life Opportunity from my phone before I went to sleep last night and this morning it was on my phone again on March 30!"

We share our disbelief about what has happened. How is it possible for a cell phone message to appear, be erased, and re-appear? But then we recall Irene texting me in the middle of the night and we now know that anything is possible.

Over the next few weeks Anne notices that whenever she tries to schedule a client for March 30 or 31, they are unavailable. After several attempts, she decides to leave those days open for whatever might be coming.

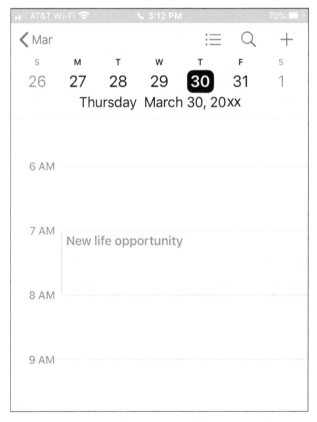

A message for Anne—new life opportunity

The weekend before March 30, a chance encounter at an art show finally gives Anne the insight she needs to act on Irene's messages to create beautiful art through her breath using ink. Patrick and Anne attend an artist's event in a large warehouse that houses many galleries of local artists. She talks with an artist who uses ink to create art, and suddenly she knows what she needs to do.

She calls me the following day and excitedly tells me, "Reese, I know what the ink and plastic is now, and I just went out and bought all of the supplies I need to try painting with my breath!" The tone in her voice tells me that her spark is back—something has opened in her and she is motivated and on track with what she must do next. She has already started playing with the paints, and all appointments are canceled for March 30 and 31.

Wednesday Morning—March 30

I am working on a client file while sitting in the big green chair in my living room. Suddenly the TV turns on by itself. I know Irene is here.

I ask, "What?"

I hear Irene's voice clearly in my head: "Be alert—big changes are coming—it is a New Life Opportunity for Anne."

Irene Critiques the First Lovitude Soul Paintings

Anne spends two full days creating her Lovitude Soul Paintings and a few days later, I am writing in my journal with Irene who has some guidance for me to pass along to Anne.

IRENE: Tell Anne she's on track—the new work is beautiful. It's a two-muffin morning. Many conversations are coming from all kinds of places. Let souls breathe through her.

I can't wait to see how she paints me. Match my breath—she can sit with me and we can breathe the art … ironic since I had that nasty lung cancer!

Share art with Sarah—all in good time—she's not ready yet—give her breathing room (Ha!).

Ask Anne, where is the iridescence? Just a nuanced glimmer. Your signature. So subtle it attracts the imagination.

ME: Irene, why are you telling me this?

IRENE: You are my scribe—I write through you. You can discern what I'm saying—you know everything about me—you're my voice. I am so grateful that you see me and know I'm here. I'd DIE (Ha! No pun intended!) if I had to wait around for people to know I'm here. More to tell …

Sometimes there are huge gatherings with our guides and angels. It's fun. We talk about ways we let our loved ones and others know we are here to help. It's absolutely amazing, the signs people here give. So clever: suddenly changing the temperature, wind, leaf rotations (Ha!). And I have been telling some of them about how I'm spreading my love of color out into the world through colorful language (You!) and the colorful soul paintings by Anne.

She can put the paints by photos of us to get the paints to respond. *Hidden Messages in Water; please infuse.* (This is a reference to the famous experiments conducted by Dr. Emoto who studied the impact of positive and negative energy on water crystals. Anne studied with him during her Master's program.)

What else? Well, I'm happy all the time here. Even when I observe sadness from humans, I can energetically comfort them. You can teach people to just settle down and TUNE IN! Can't they see us? We are literally *right* here!

A fun thing here is learning about everything people have been through and we talk about how we lived and died, and people like to tell really funny stories. They talk about fumbling around in life—if only they knew who was there for them.

Earth is like "Pin the Tail on the Donkey." You have a blindfold on, and everyone is shouting out what you should do—which way to go—and it's so easy to lose confidence, feel ridiculous, and unsettled.

Did you know angels and guides over here can see perfectly? We can't make you go directly to the right place, but you can ask us to guide you.

ME: So, if everyone did that, there would be one hundred percent perfection in everything we do?

IRENE: But, there's also a wildcard. You come to earth with a secret mission—you are there to learn something. So that is the challenge. You are intermittently reinforced. You ask and we give—but not always. You sometimes want what you think you want—but we see consequences and may send you off course.

We'll be there but we will not necessarily give you the results you desire. If we did, you wouldn't learn patience, sharing, trusting others.

What are your plans today? Be effortless, allow the flow. Come see me. Talk to me.

Blessing the Lovitude Soul Paintings

Once Anne starts painting with her breath, everything about her approach to creating art bursts wide open. Her original small watercolor pieces are instantly replaced with stunning paintings on large sheets of clear plastic in vibrant, peacock colors. They quickly manifest one after another, and it seems she can produce beautiful finished paintings in minutes. I am astounded and in awe of how quickly the paintings appear. She is equally amazed and so grateful for the gift.

Before she begins each Lovitude Soul Painting, she blesses the painting as Irene has instructed her to do. She sprinkles drops of dōTERRA® essential oils directly onto the plastic sheet. These essential oils are created from many natural sources, including flowers, leaves, seeds, nuts, fruits, and tree bark, and are known to provide physical and emotional benefits. She also blesses the painting with drops of Frankincense and Myrrh.

Anne is focused and quiet as she blows through a straw to move the ink that has been dripped onto the clear plastic background. Instantly she transforms the ink into vivid images that burst with color and energy. Exotic flowers, swaying trees, glimpses of the night sky. I notice that she blows through the straw to activate the ink in continuous movement—without judging or taking time to step back and decide what is needed next to add to the piece.

She is as happy and relaxed as I have ever seen her. Creating the paintings appears to bring her to life in the same way that they ultimately will inspire others.

In the coming weeks and months, she devotes hours to this new passion and finds that the best results come when she is relaxed and "not trying to create a painting!" She worries that others might think that she is an artist and she will have to confess that she is *not* an artist and, in fact, has never studied art.

Momentum is building, and slowly the lower level of her home fills with painting after painting displayed on walls, scattered across the floor to dry, or already framed and propped two- and three-deep against all available wall space.

In the meantime, I continue to journal with Irene, and she provides messages for me to deliver to Anne about modifications to the art. The irony is not lost on us that Irene was never an artist herself; she would have no idea how to create this artwork, much less instruct anyone else on how to do it.

First Painting - Sobbing Universe

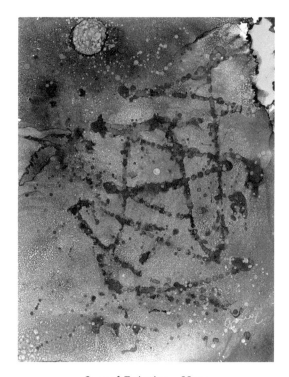

Second Painting - Hope

Peace Garden

A First Glimpse of the Paintings

In early April, I stop at Anne's house to see her paintings. We are in the lower level of her home where she has created her art studio. I am absolutely stunned. There are peacock-colored Lovitude Soul Paintings everywhere—drying on tables and other free surfaces, a few strewn across the floor. They are beautiful and so alive with energy and brilliant colors. I cannot believe how many there are … Twenty? Thirty? Fifty? She has been painting in every free moment she has, and the paintings seem to come alive one after another. She assigns a name to each painting and tells me she is inspired by the painting itself and the name simply comes to her.

This is the Anne I know best—the one who is excited and inspired and grateful for all the gifts that life and God have provided to her. She speaks of her amazement that she can create this beautiful work only using ink and her breath. She admits that she first tried painting just with her breath—no straw—and was instantly exhausted. No paintbrushes are involved. There is no thinking ahead of time about what she will paint—it simply flows from her.

The Five A's Activation Process

As we marvel at how quickly she has manifested her Lovitude soul paintings, Anne tells me about a dream she had about the Five A's Activation process.

"Tell me more," I say.

Anne begins, "I learned that the Five A's are about connecting with the spirit world and then responding to the messages we receive. They are the steps we need to take to move from messages we receive to action we will take to bring the spirit messages alive in this world."

She tells me about how the Five A's appeared to her in a dream as a process we can each embrace:

1. ASK—be willing to ask for spirit connections.
2. ALLOW—allow the message in, in whatever form it comes.
3. ACCEPT—accept the message as it is delivered.
4. APPRECIATE—be grateful for the connection and the message.
5. ACT—act on the insights and/or the information received.

Anne begins, "First, if we want to communicate with our loved ones who have passed and our guides, we must be willing to **ASK** for the connection. Many of us wait and pray that someday we will receive a message, but, as Irene tells us, if we ask, our loved ones and guides can hear us asking and that may trigger messages from them that will help direct us."

She goes on, "Then we must **ALLOW** the connection to come in, in whatever form it comes. Sometimes, we dismiss the messages that we receive, thinking that our mind is making them up—and then we don't follow up on them." Anne reminds me that it was tough allowing in the messages that she was to create large paintings on plastic using her breath when she is "NOT AN ARTIST." Her fear-based ego put up great resistance to the idea.

Thoughtfully Anne adds; "Once we ALLOW the messages to come, we need to **ACCEPT** them as we receive them. It might be convenient to change the content of the messages—but we must trust that the messages have come in exactly as they were meant to be received. We do not need to know the reasons."

Because it is such a gift to connect and receive messages from the spirit world, Anne talks about the importance of being grateful for the connection. "**APPRECIATE** the connection and the messages that come and more messages may follow. It's work for the spirit world to get through to us humans and so it is important to acknowledge their efforts."

"Finally," Anne says, "we must **ACT** on the insights or information we receive. Bring the message alive. If we don't, what is the point of the communication?"

Drinking hot tea, we spend time looking at the Lovitude Soul Paintings from the perspective of the Five A's and it is apparent that the process works.

Anne recalls asking Irene, when she was in hospice, to be sure to send us messages. Then, one year after her passing, Irene communicated with Anne to begin creating these large painting with her breath. "Imagine if I hadn't allowed those messages—if I had just dismissed them as something I had made up?"

I playfully remind Anne that it took her three months to fully allow the messages in!

We both concur that acceptance is a crucial piece of the process.

Anne says, "It was so hard to understand and accept what Irene was telling me to do. I'm NOT an artist and I've never heard of ink paints or big plastic sheets to paint on—let alone blowing the paint around with a straw! That's crazy!"

We talk about how grateful we are that we have built this strong connection with Irene. Anne knows how blessed she is to have received guidance to create these beautiful Lovitude Soul Paintings and she is so glad that she acted on the messages she received. I notice a joy in her that wasn't apparent for months while she was wrestling with what to make of the messages. Now it is clear that the soul paintings were meant to come into existence for the sheer joy that they produce. We agree that they are Divinely inspired.

Sharing the Spirit World

By mid-April, Anne is busy painting in every spare moment, and I spend much of my time working on the book. One day I sit down to journal with Coach and some interesting ideas percolate about sharing messages about the spirit world.

COACH: We'd like to talk to you. There are many of us who come as Coach to you. Those of us who have been with you since birth have always been around to lead you. Some of us have joined in or come and gone in your life. Is that confusing? I talk of *Us* as though we are one—which we are because we blend. Instead of a plain piece of cake, we come as cake with raisins and walnuts and spices.

We speak as one voice to you.

We have things to say this morning about you claiming your birthright. We always have your back and we want you to use your voice to lift others into the higher realm. Get past fear. Know there is always help.

These are scary, fear-based times for some. People have been tortured and killed since the beginning of time. You are a peacekeeper.

Keep YOUR personal agenda out of the way. Let us speak through you so the world hears you loud and clear. You truly bring great news.

Here is a thought for you. Where are the people who must hear our message? Go there. Start with a group. Sit in a circle. It's story time. Now open them so they share what they see and know. Everyone needs to remember their story.

Do not concern yourself with the stories of fear and oppression. They will always be there. You only need to bring lightness. Show our love, support, encouragement.

A great wind comes to blow evil away … and then there will be warm sunshine and love.

We want you to step up your game. Clear your surroundings, empty your distracted mind, then do the task at hand.

Finish the book and we will give you another and another.

Teach others how they can be self-reliant, by calling on us when needed. If we just team up, maybe this earthly shifting about would change. You are hard at work. Each day, there will be a new surprise, another veil will lift, more information will come in.

Be our translator of the amazing, healing, loving, energy we hold. We are a powerful force, a fierce friend. We give support and messages to humans with a silly sense of humor and a commitment to serve.

More Support from Irene—April

Some days I feel like I am on an emotional rollercoaster, writing this book. One minute I am confident and focused, sure that I am on the right track. The next minute I am wondering how I ever got such an assignment. I wonder if the messages I am receiving can be clearly communicated with others.

I open my journal to see if Irene is available to talk with me.

ME: Irene, are you here?

IRENE: Reese—don't worry so much. I told you we're helping. I know you've been busy and distracted—a little down. Planets or something. Anyway, I'm here—we're here. Tell my story, please. Do it for Sarah—she needs to know. And let them know about what we can do from the other side.

We're going to send some people your way to deepen your learning even more. Get help on this book.

ME: Irene, I really miss you here. I know we can talk whenever, but it would be such fun if you were around here. By the way—Sarah loved the flowers. (I sent pink roses to Sarah at the direction of Irene.)

IRENE: Don't slow down. You've got momentum. Brew a big pot of coffee.

ME: How many places can you be?

IRENE: As many as I want. I can be with you, Sarah, Anne, many friends, those beautiful children in Syria. No task is too big—though I am an apprentice here. I have to learn discernment because I still want to save people. I'm on the smaller jobs but you wouldn't believe what's possible. God is real and splits into many entities (like Oscar statues!) and goes everywhere at once. He can cause total transformation on a huge scale. Like maybe make some more planets and places to visit. It's so bright here and so wonderful! It'll be here to greet you someday.

I close my journal and remain in reflective silence. How did I end up here? I am myself—but a different self. I see and I believe in this spirit world connection, and it matters. I am an ambassador with messages I want to share. I am an instrument now—a ballpoint pen telling an amazing story. Irene is always around, no matter where I am, and it is Divine.

Life in Constant Motion—May

The stresses in my life seem to be piling up on me and I am out of sorts. I'm allowing myself to get way too caught up in daily drama, world events, fear in general. And now my technology is out of whack too. My trusted laptop computer has died and the hassle of finding a new one, transferring files, and getting back on schedule with my clients is taking its toll. Time has been flying by for the last week or so, and I have not been meditating or slowing down.

I wake up early on a May morning and open my journal to write.

ME: Irene, I know you've been waiting for me—I've been so stressed about technology and world events.

IRENE: No worries—you need to slow down—take care of yourself. That's all you have to do. Just go to the still quiet place inside you for a while to recharge. Unplug—get centered. It's a beautiful day. You're in a beautiful world.

Sarah is waiting for you to reach out. See her place. Ask her how she's been.

ME: Are you disappointed that I've stepped away from the book over the past month?

IRENE: No! Absolutely nothing to worry about. The story is already there. You are the scribe. You need a clearing of time—create it. Things will flow just like art does for Anne. Make it your priority and so it will be.

ME: What can you teach me today? I'm open.

IRENE: How about the connection piece? I am constantly in a big love-connecting energy bubble. I am NEVER alone. I am unique and belong to everyone—everywhere. This is home—everyone belongs.

We're sprinkling love seeds and inspiration on everyone on earth. If people wake up it's all there—a game we play. We SEE and throw big hints. Wish others well—light the path for you and for them.

Manchester (where there was a recent school shooting) was a tremendous loss—children died, and the bomber was a child as well, a lost soul yearning for recognition and acceptance. Dark energy … challenges to the system … but all souls are one. We heal them, love them back to the center where all is good.

We're going to take good care of you. You've been busy, worried, acting all earthbound. Forget it—it's just drama. Open up, look out to the world, lend a hand and a heart.

ME: Irene, what would I do without our connection? You are my friend on the other side now. My lifeline to the afterlife. I appreciate the connection so much.

IRENE: Meet up with our coworkers this afternoon. I'll be there, you'll feel better. But first, take another nap, you're exhausted.

Anne manifests her paintings so quickly! Family caregiving is slowing her down. It's okay—time for her to really appreciate and love the work she is creating.

Each piece has a voice—a song. I am infusing a bit of the eternal through the energy—whether that's her breathing, the way the paint lands on the page, the moments of distraction.

These are collections of wonder … new life … flowers … everything growing and thriving. Hope always that love grows. Pictures that inspire creation and possibility in others.

Take care of earthly stuff—bills, setting things straight, cleaning—and then you have clarity to do your real work.

You and Anne offer support to others—and we have different work for you—bigger stages—more diverse audiences.

You will be called together in big rooms—conferences—to stimulate how others think. Not just how they lead, but to open themselves to deeper conversations.

We lead, open doors. Look for the hints, follow the leads, be aware.

ME: What else? There's more.

IRENE: Shifts are coming—no worries. Shine bright. You are a docking station—a lighthouse. See both worlds—coax darkness into light.

Hand over the reins—trust—allow yourself to step back and follow for a change! Be open—you don't have to do it all. Be like the flying geese—lead—then allow others to lead. You will not be disappointed. You will not be left behind. Attract the good ones—have each other's backs. It's what we do here. It's a beautiful thing.

Say, "I have your back. I'm here for you," and that will attract those who are here for YOU! Think about it—this is a huge lesson about committing. Let others know you have their back. HA! Such small issues in the grand scheme of things.

This is a new way to think. ONLY work with those who have your back one hundred percent.

Pink Roses for Sarah—June

When I tell Anne about the message from Irene and the pink roses I sent Sarah from her mom, Anne is inspired to paint a beautiful picture, titled *Pink Roses for Sarah*.

We stop at Sarah's for a tour of her new home (which she has decorated with the same impeccable taste her mother had) and Anne offers her the painting.

The painting will hang in Sarah's bedroom beside the many photos of Irene from Sarah's childhood to adulthood. There is a perfect spot on the wall of her bedroom and the painting is the ideal size.

We spend time chatting in the warm sun out on the patio. We tell Sarah stories about the messages and the art, and she listens with an open mind. It warms my heart to see how well Sarah is doing, and I am grateful for her friendship and connection.

Pink Roses for Sarah

Everything Is a Lesson

Anne is a highly sought-after speaker at small and large events and conferences all over the country. She is an expert in LinkedIn and social media, with an inner drive toward visionary and futuristic thinking. People are drawn to the keen insights she offers and her engaging style.

A few weeks ago, she was asked by the head of an association for financial and accounting professionals to give an early morning presentation at their annual conference. The topic: Artificial Intelligence and the Increasing use of Technology to Supplement Daily Life. She asks me if I will come along for moral support.

Anne is a brilliant and inspiring presenter—I've seen her in action many times. But I sense this is going to be a big challenge. This audience will be a different group than she is used to—detailed, technical, prone to focusing on the moment. She is prepared to inspire them to act on the endless possibilities to expand their businesses through artificial intelligence. They may wonder what they have gotten into so early in the morning.

We are in the conference room by 6:15 a.m. to prepare for the presentation. I notice that the room has been set up with round tables to seat hundreds of attendees, though we suspect there will be a much smaller crowd. I have a strong hunch that there will be no one sitting in the first few rows.

Sure enough, 7:30 a.m. rolls around and just a handful of coffee-laden attendees have settled into chairs at tables in the back few rows. I try to gently coax them forward, but they're not having it.

As Anne works her way through her robust presentation, I notice that hardly anyone seems interested in the topic. Their response has nothing to do with Anne—this is just not an area of interest for this group. Cell phones are out at every table and there seems to be great interest in checking email, sending notes, setting up business meetings.

In the meantime, Anne is trying her hardest to keep this group engaged and I watch as she slowly but surely comes to the realization that most of these attendees could care less about the topic she is presenting.

When the agonizing hour is finally over, Anne is ready to leave it all behind. Frustrated at having spent hours of time and energy researching and preparing this presentation, she wonders aloud if she should be pursuing a new track.

The next morning, I open my journal and can already hear Irene talking to me.

IRENE: Hey, Reese! FINALLY you can write today. I'll keep you inspired and things will click. Tell Anne we sent her that (presentation opportunity) her way yesterday so she can say ENOUGH! Just a dentist appointment. Get it out of the way. Don't waste time with the small stuff. Good to be in the great halls but fill them with warm bodies, open minds and hearts, leaned forward in their chairs.

Tell people your story and then they tell *their* story. Get the lights going … avoid the dark muddy places. Not your place any longer.

Tell YOUR stories now … time to share the deep stuff … both of you. We have assignments—people you are to meet. Co-create with others. Find the right places … conferences on enlightenment. What is the value of soul expression? HUGE! Everyone hides it. I did too … but my actions came from love.

Love your audience … all of them. Remember your bright light …you connect.

We're sending extra doses of light now … glowing beings … magnetic … you attract. No ego … let go of any of that nonsense. It's lower energy.

Crystals are surrounding you. Look around. We're lighting it up for you. Be at ease.

Tell Anne to lie on fluffy pillows and listen to soothing music. Have her quiet down and listen to me. She is breaking out from a box she built around herself.

Troubled Waters

One day in mid-June, I walk in the side door of my house and step into a puddle of water seeping from floorboards in the half-bath. I also hear Niagara Falls. Something is happening and it is not good.

I dash to my main floor bedroom and the carpet is soaked. Water is overflowing from the toilet in the connecting bathroom and I realize that it has likely been running for the five hours I have been gone!

Bolting down to the lower level of my house, I hear water pouring from the storage room ceiling and discover that the carpet is soaked. Several ceiling panels are now strewn about the floor, and there are boxes and boxes of stuff (Christmas décor, old photo albums, clothes I might fit into someday, random discarded house-wares, and who knows what else) that are now soaked. Around the corner in the guest bedroom and bathroom, the ceiling looks ready to cave in and water is pouring from the ceiling lights.

Over the next several months, I have huge room fans brought in to run 24-7 and move clothing and furniture from one place to the next while repairs are taking place. I have ceilings and carpets replaced, the main floor bathroom retiled, walls painted throughout most of the house, and have the wood floor sanded throughout the dining room and living room. These tasks, on top of computer trouble and a growing caseload of clients, are testing me to the limits.

I am supposed to be writing a book!

COACH: We were wondering when you would be back for some moral support. Always trying to push through—surmount the obstacles. Do it yourself. You've had big tests this past few months.

You don't control what happens around you. Yes, maybe you manifest, but then you get caught up in things that bring your energy down.

Funny you wanted to meet us again. As if we've gone anywhere! Irene is front and center right now, guiding you.

IRENE: Reese, it was all just a funny lesson on letting go … on being in the flow. You have exhausted yourself … trying to win the race … just like on the Camino! That is so earthly. I'm glad to be done with it. Less pressure. Now I get to help you.

Be sure to ask us for help! We can do incredible things. Move water. Did we set up that tank overflow? We can stop your technology if it will get you to slow down and remember. I've missed talking with you, but see that the lesson took a while—computer, copier, flood, TV— laugh it all off! There are gifts in all of this. You have a fresh, spruced up place. Now it's clean and ready if you ever need to move.

Release the stories that hold you back! And wrap yourself up in not knowing or remembering. Ocean, currents, rivers, moonlight … not a care in the world. Peace, joy, love, no constraints … so lovely, summer nights … self-love.

Learn it. Be it. Teach compassion and empathy. Those who are ready to hear are your audience. Take a walk out in nature. Look for signs. Be led!

Hot Mess Garden

Chapter 14

Lovitude Soul Paintings
Go Public—Summer

Anne's First Showcase

In June, Anne receives an incredible opportunity to showcase her Lovitude Soul Paintings at an open house for clients of a well-known executive search firm in Minneapolis. It is the first public display of her work and 150 guests have been invited. She will demonstrate her soul painting process, while we share the story of how the work has been inspired by Irene. There will be 100 original paintings, prints, mugs, and hundreds of Lovitude cards for sale. Thousands of dollars will ultimately be donated to charity after the event.

The open house is held in an old warehouse near downtown, with cool, contemporary offices scattered throughout the building. Anne and her family and friends have spent the previous day meticulously hanging one hundred large framed prints down the long, empty white-walled hallway leading to the suite so that the hallway now resembles an art gallery, and the walls have come alive with color.

Anne tells me that it took several car trips to transport the paintings to the warehouse. As she was loading her car for yet another trip, she was suddenly plagued with self-doubts about the upcoming event. As she was driving, she spoke out loud to Irene in exasperation, "Irene, if you really want me to do this, then you had better send me a sign because this is a lot of work! Plus, these are my peers and I don't want to be embarrassed!"

As she was unloading paintings from her car, a young guy working in the facility came out to help her. He told her how much he liked the paintings and she asked him what it was about the paintings he liked so much. He told her "the peacock colors"! In an instant, Anne recalled Missy's words from Irene in the December reading that she was to paint in peacock colors. This was just the sign she desired to know she was exactly where she needed to be.

Anne's first public demonstration

The crowd seems to engage with the art immediately and many guests comment on their great joy and excitement at seeing the vibrant paintings. The atmosphere is upbeat and, while Anne demonstrates Lovitude Soul Painting, the crowd is mesmerized with her process. The most stunning painting emerged from that event. Anne names it "Life of the Party," a perfect tribute to Irene.

Life of the Party

A Debrief with Irene About
the Lovitude Soul Painting Event

The following morning, I wake early, knowing that I need to journal with Irene. I have a sense that she has things to say about the previous night's event.

ME: Irene, what did you think about the show?

IRENE: Can you believe it?! Wonderful—beautiful—they are listening. Tell Anne to guide the souls in the room to connect with the art and the spirit world. Light switches went on in some people who came.

The story will support Anne's work—so now you're helping two friends! You're good with stories.

Come back up here. You've been so earthbound. There is more to learn. Honestly, Reese, it's so amazing to go from there to here in the blink of an eye.

ME: Do you have messages for Anne?

IRENE: I'll be at the IANDS conference in a few weeks (the International Association for Near-Death Studies annual conference). Many others will be there too. Watch for openings and partnerships and reasons to go deeper. Pay ATTENTION. You are wanted at the table—both of you. Soul sisters journeying together—hold space—I'm always there. I'm touching lives from the other side. I hear the deep stories that you have not yet heard. I clear space so those people who are ready hear you.

The art bursts with love—people feel it—the heart of Anne. She lives gratitude.

Tell Anne to bring paints to the conference. Paint while speakers channel—plant our messages. Love is coming in waterfalls—lines going everywhere. From heart to art! Ha!

You bring them to our intimate story … gather by the fire. *Read my words.* The ones who remember will be most moved. They will feel blessed by the art.

The voices are in the water. Sit by the falls … listen, paint, remember, transform the whispers it's so easy, so beautiful.

Big journey ahead for both of you. The story is traveling before you. They wait for you in many places.

Anne's art—OUR art—is soaring.

A Few More Thoughts Pre-Conference

One day a few weeks before the IANDS conference, Anne calls me in the middle of the day. I can feel the energy coming through the phone and can tell from the sound of her voice that she has something exciting to share.

"You're NOT going to believe this!" she exclaims. "You know that for months I've been taking my paintings to a high-quality printer to transfer the paintings from plastic to paper. This great guy works with me and his shop has kind of a nondescript name. So, I told him that I'd always wondered about the name of the shop and he turned and casually said, "That's not actually the true name of my business. The real name is NEW LIFE OPPORTUNITY—inspired when I lost my job and decided to take a new direction."

We are both delighted and amazed, quickly recalling the New Life Opportunity notation on Anne's cell phone on March 30. We still cannot believe all the messages we receive and the synchronicities that let us know we are on the right path. We are beyond excited to delve into what people experience when they leave earth and go to the spirit world.

Anne is bringing her paint supplies and has packed as many Lovitude prints and cards as she can stuff into her suitcase. We have no agenda other than to learn, meet new people, and tell our story about Irene and Lovitude Soul Paintings to whoever is interested.

That evening I take a few minutes to journal with Irene.

ME: Irene, I've been feeling your presence all day. What's up?

IRENE: So excited to be with you guys this week. Everyone is eager to hear and share. So are the two of you. Beautiful art. Bring "Life of the Party." Tell the story. Exhibitors want to see colorful stories. It is so beautiful here. I'm amazed at everything.

You have the secret sauce—it's me! Ha! Let's go on the road. Go deep into all meditations. Pay attention—I will unlock some knowing for you. It's 1-2-3 easy.

The sky will be beautiful. Be sure to look up. Rushing waters there … nature … basics … UNPLUG!

Be available! You are witnesses—validators.

Anne is going to be so amazed and grateful. People are waiting to meet her. Be very present to people connecting with the artwork that will draw them into the spirit world. Participate in raising energy consciousness. Be AWARE. Can't tell you enough … we're working on synchronicity … moving energies … every story matters … it's a hand-selected crowd. Healers, teachers, lightworkers. Energy will rise.

Get clear: you and Anne are together with this crowd for a reason. The road opens before you. Follow your instincts … reach out … others have seen what you do not yet see. Embrace everyone.

Rise early … go outside … do a morning meditation … ask for what you want to know. Answers are there. Discern who knows—they will be mingling in the crowd. Build the net … gather the energies. No coincidences … we're working on it. We're the emcees, the concierge.

Nothing is too silly. Too light. There will be an unexpected opening. There is one hundred percent gratitude for Anne from everyone.

Write to me … make time. I will tell you more. Maybe I'll pick up some ideas. Ha!

LOVE, LOVE, LOVE that we are doing this. As excited as at Costa Rica.

IANDS Conference

We arrive at the IANDS conference hotel and the first thing we notice is that there are small waterfalls scattered throughout the property. How did Irene know?! Anne thought she would need to drive to the mountains to find a place to paint. Now she will have time each morning to sit by the water and be inspired.

After the long journey to Denver, I am finally settled into my hotel room. I know I need time to unwind from the travel and I am filled with the energy surrounding me in this hotel full of people who will be studying near-death experiences and after-death communication, all events that provide glimpses of the spirit world.

I sink into the armchair, grab my journal, and with my eyes closed and in a relaxed state, I begin.

ME: Who's here?

IRENE: Everyone—Grandma, Grandpa, Dad, Luella, Michelle, Me … we're all here. Listen! We're excited! We're telling all of our stories through speakers and the people you converse with.

Look for messages of the afterlife everywhere! It's a scavenger hunt. People have glimpses—story after story—we will help the storytellers reveal even more.

Tell everyone … share the art. It is the manifestation of our messages. Isn't it beautiful? Like the great cathedrals and the moving music and brilliant art all at the same time.

Thanks to Anne. She is spreading so much love. Her art flies everywhere!

ME: Coach, are you here?

COACH: Of course! Who do you think we all are? We ARE Coach. Remember, there is no separation here. We are one. My messages are no greater and no lesser than others'. And we are more powerful than you could ever imagine.

Here is a story: Someone walks through a painful, grief-filled life. They maybe fall off a cliff or get into a car accident and die. Then they come here and see and are forever changed.

ME: Why did you arrange this so Anne and I could both be here?

COACH: Twin flames, twin sisters. You each have the other's back. You hear things differently.

Go way deep into the experiences. That is why you are here. Get up … go outside … walk … connect with nature. Use powerful attraction energy. Manifest what you want to learn. Who do you want to see? These are your peers—open to them.

Show gratitude always. It's the secret sauce—the frosting on the cake—the glue that brings everyone together in harmony.

Be mindful. We are leaving hints and messages for you everywhere. One message at a time.

Beams of love for you … we're cheering from over here. This is exactly where you need to be. It's your moment—your debut. Tell them how wonderful and amazing each one is. They are crusaders carrying the torch for love, for truth.

Now, it's time for you to go outside, take the journal. Maybe you have questions. WE are here throughout.

Thank you for being an ambassador on earth.

ME: Blessings and love.

Experiences Galore

The four-day conference flies by in a blur. There are amazing keynote speakers, fascinating workshops, and a room I can stop in at any time to have one-on-one conversations with people who have had near-death experiences, some years ago, and are open to talking about them as though they happened yesterday.

There is a bookstore filled with great books written by those who have had a near-death experience, as well as books written by other renowned spiritual leaders. There are opportunities to sign up for sessions with healers, psychics, and mediums.

Everywhere there are great conversations to participate in. Conference attendees easily welcome others to join in whatever discussion they are having.

From day one, there are electrical problems that continue throughout the conference. I am not surprised to hear from attendees from previous years that the spirit world knows how to manipulate electronics and they want us to know they are here! In the evenings, keynote speakers set up their PowerPoint presentations for the following day and sure enough, the first slide projected on the screen in the morning is out of order. It is not unusual to see lights flicker during workshops or go out completely.

Luckily, Scott, the Master of Ceremonies (see chapter twelve, *A Chance Encounter*), keeps the speakers on schedule, the attendees informed of events, and all of us entertained by his humor and quick wit.

Scientists discuss current research on the brain and consciousness. In the past twenty-some years, there has been significant research on the topic of near-death experiences, with new insights coming daily. The physicians, nurses, hospice workers, and other healers share deep experiences of the afterlife that they hear from the patients they serve.

And everywhere there are the stories. The attendees of this conference want to talk and tell their stories in this safe and open environment.

Anne and I talk to many attendees and give away Lovitude Soul Painting cards when we share our story.

When we learn the term *after-death communication* (coined by Bill and Linda Guggenheim), it is a lightbulb moment for us. We finally have a name to call this journey we are on.

Late Saturday afternoon, I am reaching conference overload and have retreated to my room for a quick nap. Suddenly I hear a loud pounding and when I open my door, Anne bursts into the room. "Reese! We have to go down to the bookstore with the cards and prints right now." Breathlessly she tells me, "I was watching a movie in one of the workshops and the movie took place on a peacock farm! I know it's a sign!"

We grab the rest of the cards and prints, and rush down to the bookstore where we hastily set up a display table and two chairs and visit with attendees for the final forty-five minutes that the bookstore is open. Though most attendees are in workshops, those who stop by to see the art, make several purchases, and we donate all earnings to IANDS.

Lovitude display at IANDS conference

Abundant Love

Chapter 15

Nothing Surprises Me Now—Fall, Winter, and Beyond

A few months after the IANDS conference, while sipping strong coffee one morning, I glance at my cellphone and see there are four phone calls in a row from Irene. Nothing surprises me anymore. I realize that these are not real phone messages, but I know Irene is close by and has much more to say.

Another day, I grab my cellphone off the coffee table in the living room and walk toward my bedroom. Suddenly, I notice my cellphone screen light up. Glancing down, I see the photo I took of Irene in the *Sagrada Familia* Cathedral in Barcelona. She is waving and looking straight at me. I smile, say, *Hi Irene!* and marvel that I have hundreds of photos in my phone and this is the one that appears.

I continue to journal with Irene and one day she tells me, "There is a place here where you can pick a new life for yourself. You can try anything—just for fun. The new life is over in an instant, just like a dream. If you're in the mood, you can decide *I want this or that life* without even knowing what you're getting yourself into." Then she tells me that there is still much for her to do before even considering coming back.

One day I tell her that as I walked into a drugstore, I saw some-one who reminded me so much of her that I stared as she passed by. Irene replies, "HA! That was me. We show up like that—put ourselves into situations and places and people and objects that catch your eye and we are right there. You need to be open or you will not see us trying to attract your attention."

More Insights for the Paintings and the Book

As the months go by, Irene provides further guidance for Anne through my journaled messages. She tells me, "Anne is doing a waltz—a sweeping step forward, then back to rest and relax. She needs to seek more nature. Go to places of soulful inspiration. Watch the night sky, shine the light, and the paint will flow. We are out there and call her deeper with each breath. The paint glides and dances; like ice skaters crossing the shiny page. It is soul through breath—pieces of the light. We communicate through the strong vibrations in the art. Bursting colors in a kaleidoscope."

She continues, "Each painting holds a piece of the Divine. I am in the bright colors being blown across the page—a slip and slide for me. Look closely ... see my signature. Can you find me? I am in the art, but I don't always leave a mark. *The souls have come to be painted.* Each soul twirling and sparkling. Twinkles and whispers. Center ... breathe. Focus ... breathe. Expand ... breathe. Deeper and deeper we go. Each piece of art is an inspiration, an invitation, a sacred journey to Source. Beautiful, beautiful work. There is much more to come. We'll bring everything together. Yellow roses everywhere."

One day Irene reminds me, "Go on the road with Anne. Gather small circles for intimate conversations. Encourage people to talk—tell them all about what is real: *love, light, hope, beauty, grati-tude, brilliant color, sound , music.*"

She adds, "Everything is accelerating. Our story helps oth-ers remember what is beyond the veil. Allow the flow—no resistance—and you will be right here with us, where everything is magnificent and expanding. The human mind can't contain this place or categorize it."

Irene encourages me, "Reese, you are free to fly with the book. I'm going with you, of course. Nothing stops a work in progress. The book is chugging to the station. Crowds are waiting, filled with joy. The paintings are on and in each car. A truck will go by with a soul painting covering the whole side of the truck and we will smile: *Told you so!*"

Guidance for What's Next

As time goes by, I question Irene and Coach about what is coming next. Irene replies, "Where is there an opportunity, you ask? Everywhere. Our story quiets chatter-filled minds and pulls people in deeply. You and Anne are ready for the journey. Trust that others are lining up. We are selecting those who come to you. Have no worries whatsoever about what will happen next. Come and live on the bright side! Ha! Well, stay on earth, but tap into heaven more. All earthly desires are so small compared to what is available here."

She adds, "You need to ASK MORE! Look up. Look out. Armies of ancestors and light beings want to be put to work whenever they are needed. I'm meeting interesting beings from other places. You have no idea how this place goes on and on forever. You cannot find the edge. There are cycles and cycles expanding all the time. Others venture further and further out there. I am taking it a step at a time.

"All of us are *dying* (Ha!) for you to see us behind the curtain. Acknowledge us. We can be partners. Ask for guidance and signs. Say, *Please show me the path to my higher good*. Then be open, because it might not be what you think. Support EVERYONE. Help them all. People think way too small about what is possible. We have amazing plans here. We are with you always."

Now Coach chimes in. "You have a trumpet to blow. Do not leave earth without blowing that trumpet so everyone can hear. We fly everywhere—we clear the path. It's a movement gaining momentum. We are all around you—you will be safe. Treat this story with reverence. It is a gift. Many questions come from alert students. Stay grounded. Maybe this is not for everyone. Who cares? Physics books aren't for everyone either."

Coach continues, "Do not underestimate the gifts that come to those who are open and believe and share and know and love unconditionally. More music, laughter, creativity. Fill your heart, honor your soul. No one is alone and no one goes unscathed. It's school on earth. You are both teacher and student. Watch carefully—all is not as it seems. We sit quietly in support around you, but you must also learn. Remember, Paradise Speaks. The voice of God and angels and guides is everywhere. Pennies from heaven, the whisper of the wind, a voice that will not let you rest, a sense to go this way or that, a shimmer of light, sound in the quiet night, we are always here for you.

Coach reminds me, "The book is your teacher. Still your chattering mind! Make us familiar. We are right here for everyone. It is that simple! To make it otherwise is an illusion. You are past that—done with that. Take risks. Say yes to opportunities. Manifest absolutely everything. You want an audience? It's right in front of your eyes. For years you've strived. Now let us take you on a joyful journey. We are preparing you for more. Be sure to relax. Communicate with us. Keep in touch."

The Opening of Lovitude Studio—Fall

By fall Anne has created more than 300 Lovitude Soul Paintings and moves into the perfect studio to display her art, meet with clients, and demonstrate her painting. It is a calming and relaxing place with floor-to-ceiling windows that overlook a natural pond brimming with wildlife. The paintings adorn the walls and bring warmth and beauty to the space as do the scarves, pillows, glassware, and cards that showcase her designs.

Guests relaxing on brightly cushioned wicker chairs comment on the impact the artwork has on them. Many are deeply moved as Anne paints and we share the story of how the paintings manifest from the spirit world. People of all ages are enchanted by the process and awed at how quickly the paintings appear.

From time to time, Anne and I host open houses and facilitate "Out of This World" conversations encouraging others to share their experiences with after-death communication.

As Anne paints, we tell the story and ask questions of our guests: "Which of you here has had an experience of someone trying to communicate with you from the spirit world? How do you know who is communicating? What signs do they give you to let you know it is them? Do you receive important messages when you are communicating with them?"

We marvel at how quickly people are willing to share: "I know my grandmother is around when I smell her Charlie perfume." "My father sends me ladybugs." "My mother died, and I always see shark's teeth on the beach now and I know it's her."

Hearing the stories seems to awaken something in the crowd. We know that people long to connect with their loved ones who have passed, and we serve them by opening the conversation.

Occasionally, children visit with their parents and are mesmerized watching Anne paint. She asks them if they, too, are artists and they all affirm that they are.

She tells them "I'm just having fun and I'm never worried how my paintings turn out. You can paint however you want to. There are no rules!" She wants to make sure the children feel inspired to create authentically.

Anne's Lovitude studio

Advanced Mediumship Training

The following spring, I enroll in the next level of mediumship training with Suzanne Giesemann. There is much more to learn, and I want to test out my abilities to connect with the spirits of loved ones for others in the class. I am excited and nervous and need to remind myself that I am seeking learning, not perfection.

Irene provides guidance before the training begins: "Lots of souls here are cheering you on. Ask for any assistance you need. Speak your truth. Lighten the journey for others. I'll be there. Break past your own ego barriers. Some will cry at what they experience. Be with every emotion. You can contain all of it and pass along the pain and grief to us—we can transform it."

She adds, "Humans contain the tiniest spark, like matches that flicker and burn out, and flicker again. Here, there is the strongest light. Always on, like the warm sun—the source of huge power.

People on Earth forget to relight their match when the fire snuffs out. It's so easy really—just ask. Why don't people get that? It's so easy! Manifest, attract, be the brightest light possible. If your flame flickers, reconnect to Source. All problems and obstacles drop away. Miracles are real—you just don't see them because you don't know it is all about keeping the flame burning."

Throughout the workshop, there is rich learning and many opportunities through one-on-one practice sessions to connect with spirits who have passed and communicate their messages to their loved ones. Suzanne teaches us processes and techniques to help us build the connection to the spirit world. She is a patient and loving teacher, guiding us to explore and do our best.

I have several opportunities to build a connection to the spirit world and find in most of the practice sessions I am able to give the sitter specific information about the appearance and personality of a loved one who has passed, as well as how and when they passed. Other times the connection is much weaker, and I know that I must continue growing in my ability to hold the connection

At the end of the first day of training, I am exhausted and quickly fall into a deep relaxing sleep. At 2:35 a.m., I wake from a sound sleep to a tingling sensation on my head. Though my body yearns for me to shut my eyes and fall back asleep, I get out of bed, grab my journal and a warm blanket, and nestle into the armchair by my bedside to write.

Irene instantly jumps in. "Nice job! We were helping you SEE! Do you see that? No effort really. We drop in any time. Be sure to ask for the messengers and the messages. We're dying to tell you the answers."

Then Coach adds his thoughts, "On behalf of the council—and we ARE the council—you are to be commended! It's graduation day. You did it! Six gold stars! You're an official messenger now! You've allowed us to shift the physical out of your way so we can stand by your side and bring in divine guidance. The spirits are so grateful to be seen. They trust you. There must be trust! They won't trust just anyone. Like an adult coaxing a child, you must be patient and loving, and then the child responds. Now, do you believe what you see? Be open now to those who are grieving or feeling lost. It's the right path for you!"

I ask Coach for guidance on what I am to do next and he replies, "Oh, the need to know! You're on a path. Let it be! We'll show you where we want you to be. We'll speak with you with YOUR voice. Cool, huh? Archangel Michael will help. His voice booms loud and clear. We could put you on stage and you could speak. Tell them we're here. Expect miracles. They are everywhere."

A Lovitude Pop-Up Shop at Echo's Studio

Anne and I are invited to create a Lovitude Pop-Up Shop at Echo Bodine's studio in mid-December to sell scarves, cards, mugs, mousepads, prints, pillows, and other products. Anne will demonstrate Lovitude Soul Painting as I share our story.

Echo is an internationally renowned psychic medium, a master spiritual teacher, and a prolific author of a dozen-plus books on accessing intuition and the spirit world. She is also extremely engaging, has a big heart, and is a joy to be around. Years ago, Anne and I attended Echo's amazing Introduction to Psychic Development Class and became staunch supporters and fans from that day forward. Echo hosts meditation sessions, trainings, guest speakers, healers, and her monthly radio show in her studio. Once a month, she opens her doors to other members of the spiritual community to provide psychic readings, healing sessions, and to display their art and products.

Just a few months ago, Echo hosted Anne and me on her radio show and we were delighted to share the story of Lovitude Soul Paintings and the inspiration we receive from the spirit world. Echo tells Anne that the bold colors in the paintings are those that are found in heaven. She has seen the colors when she visited heaven during a near-death experience years ago. Echo, an artist herself, uses Anne's mugs to create colorful ceramic lamps.

A steady stream of shoppers peruses the products, chat with Anne and me, and select gifts for family, friends, and themselves. In the afternoon, Anne holds a short painting demonstration so others can see her process while I tell the story of Irene and how the paintings came to be. As usual, the crowd gathers in a semi-circle and quickly responds to questions about their own experience of after-death communications with loved ones. They are inspired by the demonstration and by the stories others are sharing.

An hour later, Anne pulls me aside to tell me she would like to have a second demonstration and asks whether I am available to assist. I am surprised she will be painting again, but a woman and her young daughter who have just arrived at the studio are interested in seeing Anne work.

Again, Anne dons her painting shirt, sets up her inks and essential oils, and is ready to begin. The young girl, I'm guessing six or seven years old, has moved her chair directly in front of the table where Anne is working. As I share the story with the audience and ask them questions about their own experiences with messages from loved ones, I notice that the young girl is engrossed in the painting Anne is creating.

When the demonstration is over, the crowd disperses, and the young girl continues to sit transfixed in front of the new creation. I quietly asked her, "Are you an artist?"

"Yes," she whispers. I smile, remembering that all children are artists.

Then I feel moved to ask her, "Would you like to see a picture of our friend Irene who inspired this artwork?"

She nods *Yes*.

As I show her the photograph of Irene, she looks at it for just a second and then glancing up at me says, "She came to me in my dream last night and told me that I was so smart and such a nice little girl. And she said I would get to meet her tomorrow and watch her paint."

Then she points to the corner right above and behind me and my heart is filled with joy as she tells me, "She's been here the whole time."

Risë, Echo, and Anne at Echo's Studio

A Final Message from Irene

Days pass quickly in the business of the holiday season. Late one afternoon, several days after the Lovitude event at Echo's, I feel the familiar warm tingling sensation on my head, and I know that Irene wants to communicate with me. It's been a while since we have journaled, and I have missed her insights. I settle into my big green chair, journal in hand, and spend a few quiet moments relaxing with my eyes closed before I begin to write.

IRENE: See, I told you how it is—now you know how to spread the word. So, so, so easy! I wish everyone knew. It's heaven over here. Ha!

I'm sending all kinds of people your way—to you and Anne. Yin and yang, fast and slow, tick-tock. There's a rhythm ... messages are delivered slowly so others can see and hear.

People saw you ... there's a glow. I'm right with you. I love it!

Everyone needs Anne's paintings so they can see and hear all the energy—the story, the paintings, you are drawing them here ... the curious, the troubled. NOT the skeptics—let me just clear them away for now—someone else can handle them.

Pack your bags. Send displays ahead. Make my book into an e-book or whatever is up with the technology.

You can tell Anne swirls with excitement and sparkles with the deep energies in the paintings.

Everywhere there is a need to know—a deep desire.

ME: How do we translate the messages from your world into action?

IRENE: One soul at a time. One soul shares with another. Then that soul shares, then it spreads. Share by asking questions. Open the conversation. People know—a small glimpse is enough to make them curious. No pushing. Draw them to you. Ask them to gather around to hear our story.

ME: Tell me more about heaven.

IRENE: Just for fun, doors appear—magic light. It's just delightful. Someone thought this up—maybe me. I open the door and I am anywhere I want to be. I'm walking the streets of Paris, boating down the river, checking out the pyramids. I am here AND there. You know I love Paris. I just transport there. No need to hassle with the airport. If I want anything I just look and there it is.

Dexter's here (Irene's cat who died several years ago). He's as talkative as ever. He was sleeping in his basket so I would know it was him.

Glad you heard that I left my body right away. Funny story: I sent that belligerent client to distract you and she didn't even know she had been given specific directions. I always knew you were around. I looked as though I was out of it—my body was out of it—but the rest of me was so aware.

You mean the world to me. Thank you for so much fun and friendship and love and laughs and goofing around. When you come someday, we'll create the pool and the noodles, and float in the warm sun and catch up and carry on with the work.

Your next book will be the stories of the art. Where it has flown. Stories of how people were comforted and became more aware because of the art.

ME: Since this first book will end here, do you have a message for our readers?

IRENE: Greetings from the *real life ... the real world*. I brought you here to hear and know and trust that your intuition is larger than a hunch. It is the keyhole to all that is real and alive. It is embracing you every moment on earth.

We're around you all the time—even in your darkest hours.

Live your earthly life by spreading joy, being joy. Bring light with you wherever you go. Heal old wounds, give love freely to everyone.

You are on earth to have fun. You must take the steps through your life and remember there is always support when you need it. You get in sticky messes sometimes or you feel lost, but remember we are always here. You are just twirling around in a water globe right now.

Clean up your messes. Figure that out, please. We might be coming back in and we'd like clean hotel rooms!

Do you know how perfect you are? Every piece. Click your sparkling red shoes and you can go wherever you want to go—see everything—create door after door after door. Open them—don't hold back. Live every day in pure joy. We embrace you and love you.

Anne and Reese, I knew I could entrust you and infuse you with messages for all. Crusaders and prophets for all that is good.

Love, love, love to you both.

Irene

On studio set for Hallmark Home and Family Show

Acknowledgements

A mystic by nature, I have been intrigued with the spiritual world my entire life. My desire to understand and experience what lies beyond what we access through our five senses has served as a light guiding me to the inner workings of my own psyche, and outward to the source of unconditional love and guidance the spirit world provides.

When Paradise Speaks is the result of hundreds of hours of journaling, month after month, capturing messages from the spirit world from Irene, Coach, ancestors, and other guides I met along the way. Because they provided continuous wisdom and encouragement, I felt guided and supported in the process of delivering this amazing story out to the world.

I am grateful beyond measure to my friend, Irene, for our twenty-year earthly friendship and our relationship that continues today. She encouraged me throughout the writing of this book and freely shared her insights from the afterlife whenever I was open to listen. She communicated to me that writing this book would become my all-consuming passion project. And so it is.

There are so many who helped bring this book to life.

To my brilliant, kind, and compassionate friend, Anne Pryor, who was with me every step of this journey; I am so grateful for our ongoing friendship and for all the hours we spent in deep conversation about the afterlife and for how we acted on the messages Irene was passing along to us. Your hundreds of Lovitude Soul Paintings, inspired by Irene, are truly "visual blessings" and proof that everything is possible. Thank you for sharing your lovely art in this book.

To Wes Hamilton, my spiritual coach and mentor, I cherish the sage wisdom you provided while guiding me through a deep meditation program during the first year following Irene's death. Because of you, I learned to meditate daily, journal about my experiences, and savor the learning that came from discovering glimpses of insight and understanding from my unconscious mind. You taught me how to build my light body and radiate that loving force out into the world. Thank for your unwavering support of me and this story that needed to be told.

To my other amazing spiritual teachers: Echo Bodine, Dr. Todd Ovokatys, Paul Selig, Suzanne Giesemann, and Missy Reno Smith, you taught me so many ways to hear and trust the still voice within. You expanded my skills in connecting with the spirit world and I honor the passion and commitment you bring to your work. You are truly inspiring.

Thank you to Nina Shoroplova, the most brilliant editor and book coach. I am in awe of your skills and attention to every little detail that makes for a great book. You are so talented, and I admire that you have helped so many people bring their books to life. Thank you for introducing me to Amit Dey for his excellent book formatting, and Geoff Affleck for his exceptional publishing and marketing guidance.

A special thank you to Irene's daughter Sarah, who granted me permission to write this very personal story right from the start.

I am so grateful that you were willing to be open to the possibility that everything I was experiencing was real. I know that your mother is always watching over you.

Finally, thank you to all the people who heard me tell this story and championed me to write it. Jana Bauer, Laurie Peterson, David Boyce, Wes Hamilton, and Anne Pryor, thank you for reading numerous drafts and providing great insights.

About the Author

Born in Minneapolis, Minnesota, Risë Severson Kasmirski, MA, is an author, mystic, and the founder of Right-Path Careers, an Executive Career and Life Coaching firm. Before founding her company, she worked in the corporate world in executive sales, marketing, and training.

She began after-death communication with her friend, Irene, within months of Irene's passing. Through lucid dreams, channeled writing, and direct communication through a medium, Risë was inspired by Irene to write *When Paradise Speaks* to share wisdom from the afterlife and help others access the guidance and unconditional love available to them from the spirit world and their loved ones who have passed.

With her friend and business partner, Anne Pryor, Risë shares the story *When Paradise Speaks* and the birth of Lovitude Soul Paintings to audiences globally.

A fun fact, Risë (pronounced Reesa) was named after an opera singer but she prefers the blues!

About the Artist

Anne Pryor, MA, is the creator of Lovitude™, and a Soul Painter, recently featured on the Hallmark Channel. She is also an internationally recognized LinkedIn Expert, Career Coach and a former executive with Lifetouch, Carlson, and Knott's Camp Snoopy at the Mall of America in Minneapolis, MN.

She was inspired through after-death communications with her friend Irene to create vivid images to activate souls. She has created more than 1,500 soul paintings using ink, her breath, and essential oils on plastic. Anne was not an artist before these messages. These paintings have been called "visual blessings" and are licensed on products distributed globally.

With friend and business partner, Risë Severson Kasmirski, Anne demonstrates Lovitude Soul Painting to audiences globally as they share the story, *When Paradise Speaks*.

A fun fact, Anne worked with Charles Schulz on the grand opening of Knott's Camp Snoopy and he is one of her guides.

Resources

PRESENTATIONS AND KEYNOTE SPEAKING ENGAGEMENTS

We welcome the opportunity to present this unique story of after-death communication and demonstrate Lovitude™ Soul Painting at conferences and events. We are available to speak on a variety of topics, including After-Death Communication (ADC), Accessing Lifeforce to Enhance Your Leadership, and Creating Through Soul.

To inquire about presentations and speaking engagements, contact us:

Risë Severson Kasmirski at rise@lovitude.com

Anne Pryor at anne@pryority.com or anne@lovitude.com

LOVITUDE™ PRODUCTS

Please visit Anne's website www.lovitude.com/products to find links to purchase Lovitude products or to License Lovitude images for products sold at retail or through e-commerce. A portion of licensing sales is donated to charity.

View Anne Soul Painting on the Hallmark Channel Home & Family Show https://www.youtube.com/watch?v=gmCB8BefH0s

LEARN MORE ABOUT AFTER-DEATH COMMUNICATION

Visit www.lovitude.com/resources for a list of subject matter experts and organizations dedicated to research and advanced understanding of ADC.

Omega Institutes -
Blue Spirit Retreat Center
in Costa Rica

Missy Reno Smith
a Midwest Medium

Say " please show me the path
to my higher good. "

Just ask. Anything.

please send me messengers and
messages. Help me be aware to
see, hear, feel, know them

CPSIA information can be obtained
at www.ICGtesting.com
Printed in the USA
BVHW090022231220
595992BV00003B/25